Business Cards

Transforming the Organization One Card at a Time

Greer · Joel

Publishing

Business Cards: Transforming Business One Card at a Time

Copyright ©2012 by George B. Lampere, Ph.D.

Published by Greer-Joel Publishing Company
1921 E. Tano Lane Mt. Prospect, Illinois 60056
www.greer-joel.com

Library of Congress Control Number:

Lampere, George B.
        Business cards: Transforming Business One Card at a Time /
        George B. Lampere, Ph.D. – 1st Edition.
                p.   cm

                                                            2012942139

ISBN-13   978-0615643878
ISBN-10   0615643876

Learn more about the author

Printed in the United States of America

For additional information contact
(847) 794-8910
E-Mail: glampere@glampere.com
www.glampere.com

iii

Table of Contents

Table of Figures

This book is dedicated to my wife, Jo-Ellen,

who could always see good things in me.

Preface

Many organizations are undergoing some sort of "transformation" to better position themselves in the marketplace, to boost sales, to improve customer loyalty, and to provide value to the shareholders, employees, and the community. Change is occurring too rapidly to remain steadfast or to make incremental improvements in hopes the success experienced from the past, with minor adjustments, will be enough to keep pace. Evolutionary change has been replaced by transformational change within organizations to survive. Transforming an organization implies a complete, often radical change in every aspect of the business. Technology has been in many cases the driver of change.

In the mid 1990s, Enterprise Resource Planning (ERP) systems integrated and automated many of the back office functions such as accounting and finance, human resources and supply chain management. These systems changed the process of how work was performed, improving the time and accuracy for financial reporting. The implementation of these systems disrupted work for those businesses not prepared for the resulting changes. These organizations also incurred additional costs including software licensing and maintenance fees, new hardware, and contracting consultants experienced in implementing these systems.

The disruption in part was due to the changes in work processes the enterprise systems brought about. During the same time period, Michael Hammer and James Champy published their book *Reengineering the Corporation: A Manifesto for Business Revolution*. This book and others like it brought to light the need to focus on business processes as the primary driver to improve quality and operational performance aided by the features and functionality the technical systems brought to bear. More organizations were examining their processes for improvement aided by the use of metrics and measures that were introduced during the total quality movement a decade earlier.

As the business processes and software applications enhanced processing time, the employees were becoming increasingly stressed. The current thinking among project and business leaders was to keep employees informed and train them prior to the change. At the same time, organizations could not afford to dedicate large numbers of employees to work on these projects that often took a year or more to implement. Employees were asked to work double duty, managing their day-to-day business while at the same time working on the project. More employees began resisting the changes both overtly and covertly, creating delays and even contributing to failures of the projects. The practice of organizational change management started to become popular in the mid 1990s, supporting top-down change. Many senior managers were not accustomed to being actively involved in the operational-level coordination, decision-making, and communication, preferring to lead by directives much like Star Trek's Captain Jean-Luc Picard's command: "Make it so."

A number of methodologies and approaches were used to manage change among employees which often created confusion to the purpose and value of managing the "people" change. The high cost of the project, coupled with the risk of meeting timelines, caused the change management activities to take a back seat in the project. Change management often was the last thing to be considered when planning the large-scale change initiative, and generally, the first thing to be cut when the budget became tight. Although change management still seems to be evolving, there appears to be an increasing acceptance and understanding for the need to manage the "people" component of the transformation. Business leaders are becoming aware of the influence the organizational culture has on the ability of the employees to adopt change. Strong unspoken rules may create barriers to think and act in new ways. Therefore, culture assessment and alignment is becoming essential to ensure the changes are implemented swiftly.

The level of complexity to coordinate and manage a large change initiative can be overwhelming for even the experienced project manager. The tendency of many North American business leaders is to jump right in and start making the changes. There seems to be little time or tolerance for planning; after all, Tier 1 consulting companies pride themselves on rapid design and implementation strategies for enterprise software solutions. With the high cost of the project, the sentiment among the business leaders is "get it done." An assumption is made that the business already knows how the changes will resolve the identified problem and how the changes will integrate with the rest of the business operations. In my experience, I have not seen that to be the case. The consulting team enters in large fashion and conducts an elaborate presentation of the project, defining objectives, roles, milestones and the project management approach. Project plans are soon developed as the team delves into the details. Then, certain things are discovered which create delays in the project. Like a cascade effect, other tasks begin to slip. The project, with its broad scope, aggressive timelines and a culture unwilling to change, is destined to make cutbacks. In my research I have witnessed scope cut by thirty percent on average to meet the time and resource requirements. As a result, the grand scheme of transforming the organization is often reduced to adding new functionality and features in a software application and training the employees how to use it. Although I may sound overly critical; there have been too many times the expectations far exceed reality.

Based upon my thirty years experience as a consultant, I have learned under fire what works, and what doesn't. It does not matter the organization's size or type of industry, the situation often is the same. I often kid that I have to enter a project wearing a flack vest and a helmet to protect me from highly resistant employees. I view every consulting engagement as a learning experience. The best learning experiences for me are those projects that have go terribly wrong. This occurs when the client organization refuses to listen to my counsel, but rather directs me to take a course of action that focuses on an activity rather than a desired outcome.

I have experienced how complex and confusing a large-scale transformation effort can become. This is one of the reasons I decided to write this book. The intent of this book is to provide a transformation approach for large-scale organizational change that is easy to understand that integrates people and organization, business process, technology, and information and knowledge management. I view each of these four areas as drivers of performance since they provide specific value to the organization. I believe that each of the four areas all have equal weight in terms of importance and consideration. These performance drivers interact with one another during the day-to-day operation of the business. As one area changes, such as a shift in a policy or procedure, other areas may become strained and will compensate to a certain degree. I call this phenomenon "dynamic equilibrium," where the system comprised of the four drivers will adjust and stabilize. Think of a child's teeter-totter: as one side goes down due to force, the other side will rise. Then a greater force is needed on the opposite side to create a balance within limits. However, when the change goes beyond the defined tolerance limit, the other performance drivers will be negatively impacted. An example of this occurrence is when new technology forces changes in the way employees perform their job. Automated workflow and triggers may greatly reduce manual administrative activities once performed by employees, which may eliminate jobs or significantly change tasks, requiring learning new competencies. This integrated performance approach ensures that the organization, business units, departments and employees are all aligned with the new business processes, enhanced by the new technologies, and influenced by the information and knowledge from the performance drivers.

This book has been three years in the making. I worked closely with many colleagues and friends to identify all of the critical activities and place them at their appropriate level. Then the challenge was to present the material in a way that would be easy to read and fun. Once I had the concept of using the cards in a poker game, it was the structure I needed to start writing the book. There was a great deal of research that went into defining each activity, which was followed by clarification and validation from many people who I consider experts in their respective areas.

I designed this book to be used in two ways. You are encouraged to read this book from end to end so that the approach and concepts can be fully understood. Then, you can use this book as a reference to identify and understand the activities that need to be addressed during your change initiative.

There are four sections in this book.

Section 1: Playing High-Stakes Poker Game. This section describes in a lighthearted way the situation that currently exists within many organizations that feel the pressure for the need to change, but may not understand what is required.

Section 2: Defining the Rules of the New Game. This section describes requirements that establish the environment to change and the approach used to drive the change.

Section 3: Learning the Meaning of the Cards. Each card in the suit is described by the name of the activity, a summary description, the level at which the activity is performed, a complete explanation of the activity, inputs required, outcomes desired, tools and techniques used to perform the task, metrics, planning considerations and validation of the outcomes.

Section 4: Planning the Game. This section describes how to execute the change initiative. Leadership qualities are stressed in leading and directing the initiative. Change champions are selected, and the stakeholders are brought together. Next the cards are dealt and sorted so that project team members understand the activities. Then the activities are integrated to ensure the performance levels are adequately covered.

The integrated approach that is described in this book can be incorporated into a traditional project management methodology. However, checking off on the completion of tasks without validating that the outcomes have been achieved should be avoided. It is tempting to just check the task off when it is complete. Remember that the secret of a successful change initiative is demonstrating good leadership, inviting others to participate, keeping it simple and having fun.

Acknowledgments

First and foremost, I would like to thank my family for having the patience with me taking on yet another challenge which decreased the amount of time I spent with them. I would like to thank my wife, Jo-Ellen, for standing beside me throughout my career and while writing this book. She has been my inspiration and motivation for continuing to improve my knowledge and moving my career forward. Most of the work on this book occurred on weekends, nights, while on vacation, and other times inconvenient to my family, Jill and Ben.

I am very grateful for the support and insights provided by my colleagues and friends. Bob Wegener took me on as a mentor and acted as a sounding board for my ideas. Gerold Tjon Sack Kie taught me a way to structure business processes, which developed into the performance levels in this book. My uncle, Bill Lamperes, provided the inspiration for using the cards that represent the various activities. Bill was a great coach to guide me through the process to create this book. Richard Cooper, III, was a great sounding board and aided in validating many of the ideas; he assisted in defining the way the game should be played. Richard Witt and Bonnell Langford provided their technical expertise and time to check the accuracy of the material in the original manuscript.

It was the dedicated work of Karen Parris who spent countless hours to review my grammar and sentence structure to make the book easy to read.

Most importantly, I would like to acknowledge my late father, George Louis Lampere, whose ever present spirit motivated and inspired me to write this book.

Section One

The High-Stakes Poker Game

Reconnaissance for Change

The telephone rang in my office precisely at nine o'clock in the morning. It was a call from a gentleman who I had been working with over the past year. "The time has finally come," he said, and he needed my assistance.

Throughout this time, we had developed a trusting association. I provided him with some insights, and then he described some of the issues he was facing. He had some preconceived ideas about what should be done to correct this mess, but I told him they would not work. There was more to the story he wasn't telling me. Now, I told him, "I need you to put your cards on the table and show me what you have before I make the decision to help." He agreed to the terms.

The day finally arrived. Entering the back room, I witnessed all of the players sitting around the table playing their same "friendly" game. They were quite uneasy when this stranger entered the room since they were not accustomed to outsiders entering their domain. Although no one questioned my appearance, they went about their task as usual. They knew I was a hired gun, as some call it, but the group had seen the likes of me come and go.

Observing from a distance, I could see that the stakes were high. In front of each player were stacks of accumulated wealth. Without a word spoken, some of the players appeared intimidated by their counterparts' massed capital as they shifted in their seats with each bet placed. In the center of the table was the pile of assets that each of the players risked, with the anticipation of winning the pot. The pile in the center had grown quite large as the game went on.

Although they called it a friendly game, there was little talk, the exception being an occasional comment, joke or snide remark. The conversations were much like strangers waiting for an event: no substance, just light talk.

Each player held his hand close to the vest, careful not to reveal guarded secrets. The players were watchful not to disclose too much information to tip others of their next move. Dark glasses disguising telling eyes to the others, each player acted in the same cautious way.

These games have been played continuously without deviation for years since their techniques have been proven successful. So, why change? But recently, the players have been aware that with each new game they have less money to gamble. Their bosses started putting the pressure on them to win and became aggravated when the take was low, or if they lost. That type of behavior was not tolerated for long because the players knew that a few losing hands would resort to a swift and painful end.

During a break in the action, I tried to corner each of the players and asked if any of them had discussed a new strategy for winning. They all had different ideas that would benefit them individually, but everyone was resigned to the fact that change now was beyond their control, citing the same barriers and placing blame on others. Some did share stories of those who once tried to make changes, but were shot down; regrettably, those individuals were no longer with us. Mostly, the players were uneasy to discuss anything with an outsider, and the individual conversations were vague or generic. Some of the players made excuses not to talk with me and went about their business.

I accomplished my task: to gather information that I would take back to the big boss. Somehow I knew that he was not going to like what I had to share with him. It would be at this meeting where I would determine if I would take the case. The information that I gathered was not new, and unfortunately, I had seen this situation played out too many times. The results are never pretty, unless, of course, the game is changed. There are many similarities that we can draw from our story as we examine the way they manage their business.

Their organization is losing the game with every hand dealt. It may be easy to place blame on a depressed economy that appears to be eroding their profits without examining how the business is conducted internally. The managers may, therefore, be the target for underperforming business and terminated unjustly, placing the blame on them rather than the state of the business. The poker game is a good analogy to describe the behaviors of business leaders who operate in a strong top-down command and control organization as the one I described. This controlling style, often referred to as bureaucracy, occurs as their business ages. The rules and procedures that govern the way these managers played the game were simply reflective of longstanding customs, even when they may not be effective or efficient. Our players have been dealt those cards the same way for quite awhile. This was the only way that the game was going to be played: business rules, policies and procedures simply were designed to reinforce those standards that had served them well over the years. But everyone knows that changes are needed. A directive did not have to be issued; the players just knew that things were not the same and something had to be done to set the business back on course. Changes had to be made, but where are they needed the most, how will it be made, and at what cost?

Why should there be change within an organization that has been around for many years and has reaped the rewards of success? Why change those things that have served them well? Certainly, there was a period when the company had gone through tough times, but they have always been able to weather through the storm. What makes this time different than in the past? To answer these questions we must start by looking at where we came from to determine where we are going and how to get there. Large organizations can be complex and difficult to change direction, but by understanding certain characteristics, we can make more informed decisions.

Organizations are much like people; we are born, we grow and develop, we mature and age, and then eventually, we die. With each stage of life, we have struggles, difficulties, or transitional problems which must be overcome. Young organizations lack the resources to go head-to-head with established firms. Therefore, the fledgling company targets weaknesses in their competition and pursues them with a clear vision. As progress is made, the organization learns and matures. Systems, processes and employees are added to support the increasing business demands. Those organizations that can no longer meet customer requirements and sustain performance levels diminish and close.

Leaders make operational decisions based upon commonly accepted beliefs about how the business delivers its products and services to their customers. When successes are recognized, their stories are shared among the employees to be emulated. Those accomplishments set the standard of behavior that will be followed by each manager. With each success, operational policies are adjusted to document the standards which employees will follow.

As the organization grows, the level of complexity increases within the business units and departments. As a result, the focus can easily shift inward, allowing managers to control their internal activities. It will take more equipment, more people, and more money to manage this complexity. Faced with diminished resources, department managers compete against one another for the needed funds. Their goal shifts to self-preservation and maintaining their resources. The players in the back room were ensuring they had sufficient budgets to support their projects or to maintain their status quo. They would risk portions of their budget to create wins in the eyes of their leaders.

The players are experienced and good at what they do. They know how the system works and how to get things done. They know how and when to take action, and when to sit back and observe. Their decisions to manage change are based upon commonly accepted practices. However, in a changing business environment, those practices are no longer effective. How did it get that way, and how do we know that the current methods do not work? In some instances, change can be swift and completely alter the way people think and behave. This type of change is called disruptive technology. It is these innovations that are so different it completely changes the way people think or use the product or service. There are many recent examples of disruptive technology. When Apple Inc. created the iStore to distribute digital downloadable music, it directly decreased the sales of compact discs (CDs). So, while consumers purchased their music online, the entire industry was turned around by Apple's iStore and had to think in new ways to attract customers and distribute music. Other examples include digital photography and the ability to take and distribute high-quality pictures on cell phones; the incandescent light bulb developed in the early 1800s dramatically changed with the widely accepted commercial use of compact florescent lamps (CFLs) and light-emitting diodes (LED) in homes and businesses; the book industry experienced a major shift when the eBook tablet was paired with Amazon's ability to supply thousands of titles to be purchased and uploaded instantly. This combination of a handy device and a simple distribution system made it convenient for consumers to purchase books, and in the process, crippled the old-fashioned bookstores; the telephone took on dramatic changes when combined with other functionality to create the smart phone, a multi-purpose, portable communication device; eTablets, or electronic tablets, changed portable computing; and data storage changed from mechanical devices to flash memory, allowing large amounts of data to be easily transported. All of these disruptive innovations can negatively impact or cause the demise of well-established companies as evidenced by Polaroid, Borders, Blockbuster, and Eastman Kodak.

Not all change is classified as disruptive. Change occurs in all industries and affects all businesses. Today, change occurs about two to three percent per month on average. This means that about every three years an organization will have to completely purge all of their information because it is outdated. Just think of the many sources from which we get information to perform our jobs: word documents and spreadsheets stored on our computers, information in various applications on the company's servers, numerous sources on the Internet, IMs, texting, e-mails, telephone, television, radio, and the list goes on. Now, with all of those sources, who do you believe provides the correct source of the truth? It is this information that decisions are based on. When we have old, incomplete or wrong information, decisions become difficult to make. Along with changes to information, software applications get upgraded within that three-year time frame. The upgrades provide new features and functionality. Administrative tasks that were once done manually are now computerized. Workflow is automated, signaling to others that a specific task has been completed within the process. The workforce itself is changing. The Baby Boomer Generation is heading towards retirement while Generation X and Generation Y are filling positions with a completely different work style and knowledge level. All totaled, the rate and amount of change can severely cripple an organization if they are not prepared to embrace change and create a culture that adapts quickly to current and future business needs.

Whether change is occurring swiftly or gradually without notice, it is altering the overall performance of the business. It is imperative that business leaders understand this phenomenon and take specific action to adapt to the change to maintain their competitive advantage. However, aware or not, the business is now experiencing pain that is affecting the survival of the company. The players around the table confirmed this through their comments and actions. The question still exists: Will I take the case to enable them to transform their organization to support change? I had to ask the big boss to lay his cards on the table. In other words, can I get the boss to recognize and admit to the ongoing pain within his organization and to create a vision of change through continued trust and support? This is a critical point, because the leader not only needs to recognize that there is a need, but also must know how to solve it. If the big boss believes that his subordinate managers are doing everything they can in hopes that the business will improve over time, then any outside assistance will be futile. Hope is not a strategy. The same is true of the vision for change. If the boss can develop a vision of the solution, then he can recognize the problem and describe the needed requirements, accept responsibility for solving the problem, and "see" the problem being acted upon. I knew that the big boss realized that his organization had issues that needed to be addressed. This was obvious. In our discussion, he knew that change was needed, and someone from the outside would have to offer a fresh, new approach. We sat down, and together we discussed how to address the problem to create an approach that would be accepted by all of the leadership team while reducing the inherent risks that are generally associated with traditional change efforts. I knew after our conversation that the big boss not only admitted to the pain within his organization, but together we created a vision he fully supported. I agreed to take on the project. What I showed him was a real game changer.

Section Two:

Defining the Rules of the New Game

The New Game Strategy

My challenge now was to introduce this new game to the players in a way in which they could relate. Even though I knew that the game was proven to be successful with past clients, these players saw themselves as unique, and it would be difficult to convince them that this new game was more efficient and effective, leading to bigger wins. In order to win this first challenge, I had to keep the basic concept of the game familiar so that the players would not feel a loss of control. There are a variety of ways to play poker besides Texas Hold'em, but knowing the fundamentals of the game makes understanding variations in the rules or process much easier and more readily accepted.

The purpose of the new game is to change the way in which people approach their work to achieve the organization's desired results. A strategy for change is merely a high-level plan based upon a defined vision and goal. Imagine yourself as a world class poker player — that is your vision and your goal is to play in the World Series of Poker tournament. Winning is not a goal, neither is making a profit. These are results and always should be considered the outcome of your vision and strategy. Your strategy would be to study the techniques of leading competitors and understand what differentiates them from the others. It is now time for the players to learn the new game in which they approach their change initiative. Leaders need to understand the strategy behind this new approach to ensure success. But before we talk strategy, we need to establish a sense of urgency, that driving force needed to motivate employees to actually work and behave differently to avoid a crisis, or pursue a significant opportunity. Our poker players knew there was a problem and have become increasing concerned. But was that enough to make the players change the game? It would take the big boss gathering a select group of senior leaders to discuss the problem and to ensure that this group not only understood the problem, but had enough power and influence to lead the change effort. Just because a manager says, "This is really important, and we have to do our best," it is really not the motivating force to drive change. The message must first come from a respected and credible source which will get the attention of all employees. Generally, this is the CEO. The selected group of leaders joined by the big boss met in a private room. Sitting around the poker table, the big boss said:

> "Gentleman, for the past three years, our company has been losing money. Our operating costs are excessive, and our margins are small. Our customers are dissatisfied and are leaving; we are at a crisis point. We have to reduce headcount by ten percent across the board to make up for the deficit. We have a year to improve our operational performance by at least ten percent. If we fail to meet those goals, we will be faced with further reductions."

Dealt the clear realities, these select leaders now have a common understanding of this compelling problem; they need to coalesce around a common vision. This vision describes what the organization will look like in the future. Imagery is very powerful and can paint a vivid picture of the business in coming years. I will describe the vision creation in the next section.

The vision statement that the leaders developed was a simple description:

> *We will be a much leaner, but highly efficient organization by next year. This will enable our employees to respond quickly to customer requirements and make work life more satisfying.*

Employees can visualize how their workplace will change. Clearly, they know that there are going to be fewer people, but those who remain will have more flexibility and freedom to do their jobs as they see fit. These changes should alleviate some of the stress and improve morale. As the plan develops, the messages around the vision are refined and clarified.

14

The strategy is a set of ideas that are implemented by the senior leadership to pursue desired strategic goals. At its most basic core, strategy is a matter of figuring out what we need to achieve, determining the best way to use the resources at our disposal to achieve it, and then executing the plan. Unfortunately, in the real world all of these things are not easily done. Adding to the level of complexity lays the political realm. Our players in the game, the business unit leaders and the department heads have a personal stake in the game. They are judged and rewarded for ensuring that their area of responsibility achieves the defined or perceived goals. Likewise, they assume the risk and are held accountable when their unit does not deliver. Their self-worth and personal basis of power is based upon achieving these goals. The pile of winnings in front of the player illustrates this point. Players may be intimidated or resent the one person who has won often. The winner can afford to take bigger risks and wield their power over others to get their own way.

Despite the politics, it is possible to identify the activities needing to be addressed in any change situation faced by the organization. The challenge is to have the leaders view the goal from an organizational perspective. The approach we will use in this game will provide a prospective of the organization from key viewpoints. An important aspect to achieve the desired goals is not the activity performed, but rather the result it produces. Operational performance should be measured in terms of outcomes, or the end result. Communication, for example, is critical during a change initiative in order to be informative and to solicit an action. Messages can be created to be clear and concise and distributed in a timely manner, but if the messages are not read or acted upon, then we did not achieve the desired outcome. It can be said that each of the fifty-two specific activities that you will soon learn about have outcomes that have a cumulative effect on the overall change initiative. What would be the collective result of each of these activities, and what sort of synergies can we gain to support our project? We want to ensure that the overall initiative follows a structured approach that is clearly understood and supported by the leadership.

To better understand this concept, we can classify outcomes into four areas:

Innovation and Adaptability: The ability for the organization to identify new, more efficient ways to perform work, and then make the necessary changes to incorporate the improvements into the day-to-day business.

Problem-Solving and Decision-Making Qualities: The way in which the organization members approach problems based upon differing viewpoints, and the freedom to determine alternative ways to make a decision based upon the situation.

Customer and Employee Satisfaction: Determining level of happiness, fulfillment and approval of the customers and the employees.

Quality of Service and Products: Establishing the perceived value to the customer, and maintaining that level consistently.

The strategic goal is to transition the organization from the change vision that was created and defined by the senior leadership to provide the workforce with the right information, delivered at the right time, in the right format to make informed decisions. The change vision is derived from the core values in support of the organization's primary mission. In other words, I want the users of this approach to be able to accomplish the organization's mission based upon the principles and beliefs that define their behaviors, in order to make appropriate decisions to perform their work. To bring about the change, the organization will create business processes that are enhanced by technology and staffed by the most qualified people, given the right information, so they will be able to make judgments that support the business.

These ideas are based upon what I believe is needed to ensure success in organizations and in the projects that they pursue. I strongly believe that the success of an organization and its ability to maintain its competitive advantage is directly related to its culture. Those behaviors can be directly measured through these defined outcomes: innovation and adaptability; problem-solving and decision-making qualities; customer and employee satisfaction; and quality of service and products. It is for this reason that the approach that I use is based upon collaboration and the integration of people and organizational systems; business processes; technology alignment; and information and knowledge management.

Although change can be complex and become quickly overwhelming, this approach is designed to simplify the many activities that need to be planned, coordinated and executed. To make this strategy easily understood by all of the players, I have identified fifty-two key activities needed to drive change and placed them into a matrix, consisting of four columns and four rows. Refer to Figure 1: The Matrix. The columns represent the drivers of performance, which are classified as People & Organization; Business Processes; Technology; and Information & Knowledge. These will be discussed in greater detail shortly. But first, I need to describe how I divide the activities into various levels.

	People / Organization	Business Process	Technology	Information / Knowledge Management
Strategic Level 1	1. Core values 2. Change Vision 3. Guiding Principles	1. Value Chain 2. Business Policies and Rules 3. Compliance	1. Technical Architectural Principles 2. Cloud Computing 3. Business Continuity and Disaster Recovery	1. Taxonomy and Folksonomy of Content 2. Social Networking Philosophy 3. Knowledge Management Framework
Tactical Level 2	1. Goal Setting 2. Performance Metrics 3. Inter-Unit Coordination	1. High Level Business Requirements 2. Identify and Document Key Business Processes 3. Analyze Business Processes	1. Enterprise Systems 2. Networks & Infrastructure 3. Technical Compliance	1. Knowledge Development 2. Knowledge Acquisition 3. Knowledge Deployment
Operational Level 3	1. Organizational Structure 2. Job / Position Design 3. Role Competencies	1. ID Business Rules 2. Detailed Business Requirements 3. Identify Activities and Tasks	1. Application Functions and Modules 2. Mobility and Accessibility 3. Technical Support	1. Reporting and Analytics Collaboration 2. Organizational and Team Learning
Functional Level 4	1. Job Fit and Selection 2. Individual Competencies 3. Rewards and Recognition	1. Work steps 2. Documented Procedures 3. Business Activity Monitoring	1. Application Configuration 2. Interfaces 3. Functional Parameters	1. Individual Learning and Development 2. Internalization 3. Problem-Solving and Decision-Making

Figure 1: The Matrix

The Approach Levels

The four rows are defined by levels of execution. To build a strong foundation, the tasks in each level must not only be performed, but their outcomes validated to ensure that the tasks accomplish what they were meant to be realized. Each layer is built upon the firm groundwork of the proceeding layer to build buy-in and support among the players and to provide direction. I have attempted to describe the meaning of each layer to help gain a better understanding of this approach.

Level 1: Strategy

Strategic planning activities are identified for each of the performance drivers. Strategy describes the reasons *why* the organization is making the change, which is described in a strategic plan. In the world of business, it is vitally important to analyze your competitors and work on your uniqueness that will set you apart from the competition. All roads will take you where you want to go; however, without understanding the big picture and developing a plan, your competition will arrive before you do.

Level 2: Tactics

Tactical planning describes *how* the task is executed to achieve the goal. It is the process of taking the strategic plan and breaking it down into specific, short-term actions and plans. Tactical planning is delegated to staff who are experts in a particular area, or who have managerial responsibilities within a specific function. These leaders who have the authority to make change can further delegate responsibility to those who are most qualified, providing input to the tactical plan. A manager within the information technology organization may offer a better insight to the features and capability of a particular software application than the CIO.

Level 3: Operation

The operational level defines *what* will be executed by providing the rules and requirements in which the business operates in a standard fashion. Detailed activities and high-level tasks supply the objectives that need to be performed to carry out the organization's mission.

Level 4: Functional

The functional level is where the detailed work gets accomplished. These functional work steps guide the employee through each specific task, such as processing payroll, assembling a component on the factory floor, or working the printer.

Each level is built from the proceeding level, creating a solid foundation in which to drive change. This will be further explained in the "How to Play" section.

The Performance Driver Tracks of Work

My concept of a performance driver may be somewhat different than what a CFO or other business leaders may think. Their analysis is generally from the enterprise view, assessing the financial indicators of the economy, industry and the market. The point of view which I wish to take is from the day-to-day business operations that takes place within a business unit. It is here, within departments, where the battles are fought and won by employees who interact with customers and know firsthand the inefficiencies and the opportunities for improvement. They can't, however, see the larger picture of how the business operates end-to-end.

I have identified four categories of performance drivers: People & Organization; Business Processes; Technology; and Information & Knowledge. Each category is both unique unto itself, yet dependent on the other categories to various degrees. Therefore, each category is significant and is equally weighted. A group of people will find it hard to work efficiently if the process is not defined. The work steps within the process may not be efficient if not for the technology which automates tasks, and information would be useless if the people did not have the knowledge and the tools to make informed decisions to complete the tasks and satisfy the customer.

There is a cause-and-effect relationship between the categories; a change in one of the performance drivers will have an effect on one or more of the other drivers. The outcome from this change to these other areas may not be positive and may also create issues that the managers may not be readily aware. Incremental changes within one performance driver can be adapted and adjusted in the other areas within a certain tolerance. An example of an adjustment may be to provide training to employees who use a particular software application that has just been upgraded to include an enhanced toolbar. I often observe change impact issues when there are upgrades to software programs that provide new features and functionality. The employees may show a decline in work efficiency until they learn how the new application functions, which generally will take several weeks before they adapt to the change. However, if the software application was replaced with something completely new, that changed business processes through automated workflow, streamlined decision-making, and changed data, for example, the impact to the people, business process and knowledge would disrupt and even cripple the business. Examples of major business disruption and even collapse were reported in the mid 1990s when large organizations implemented enterprise resource planning systems (ERP) to manage their back office functions. These systems completely changed finance, human resources and procurement processes, as well as the information they used. The Chart of Accounts used by the general ledger was often changed, thereby throwing the company into a state of chaos.

The concept that I use to describe the balance between these four performance drivers is called "dynamic equilibrium." Imagine a children's teeter-totter. When children of equal weight get on, the teeter-totter is equally balanced. However, if an adult sits on one side, the opposite side moves up, not allowing the child on the opposite side to control the motion. Within an organization, there is an equilibrium that exists between the employee's capabilities, their business processes, the technical tools used, and their information. It is dynamic because the organization is always shifting and adjusting within a specific tolerance. Going outside of those tolerances may result in increased stress which may lead to employee turnover, a decrease in quality, and other issues. These negative effects may not be viewed as being directly associated with a major change, and just dismissed. These are the reasons why we examine the performance drivers when undergoing transformational change.

People and Organization
An organization's people define its character, affect its capacity to perform, and represent the knowledge base of the organization. These

are the elements that define and support the behaviors that describe how people perform and work within their job. The tasks within this track are used to identify the barriers that exist and turn them into levers for change.

Business Process
The tasks in the business process track are designed to provide a systematic approach to making an organization's workflow more effective, more efficient and more capable of adapting to an ever-changing environment. A business process is an activity or set of activities that will accomplish a specific organizational goal.

Technology
Technology alignment helps to bridge the gap between the business requirements and technical capabilities to enhance productivity and profitability. When the technical system capabilities are fully utilized in supporting the business requirements to meet the change initiative goals, it can greatly reduce risk, improve quality, enhance cost efficiency and improve your chances for long-term success.

Information and Knowledge Management
Data becomes information when it is placed into context with a relevant topic. Information becomes knowledge when a person can use the information to make a decision. Knowledge becomes wisdom when the person can assess the outcome of the decisions that were made and evaluate if the outcomes align with their core values. The knowledge gained is collected, analyzed and turned into best practices where this intellectual capital is used as a differentiator to add value to the business, and as result, wisdom is created.

Now that we have an understanding of each performance driver track and the four approach levels, I will now describe each of the playing cards and how they will be used in the new game. The cards will be addressed in their suits. After all, you can't play the game effectively unless you know how each card is played.

Section Three:

Learning the Meaning of the Cards

Performance Driver Track: People and Organization

The Change Champion – People and Organization

Lead and direct the people in the organizational change track.

This is performed at Level 1: Strategy.

Description

One of the most significant components to winning the game is the change champion. The change champion is an inspiring leader that turns the vision into action. The task of the change champion is to use his or her leadership skills to guide and direct the activities in the people and organization track of work. This starts by thinking through the change vision in terms of how the organization should be structured and how the people will interact within that structure to support the mission. Then, the leader will describe the vision in a way that is clearly defined and understood by the employees. It is the responsibility of the change champion to influence others to achieve the vision and accomplish the mission. The change champion motivates subordinates by providing them with a deep sense of purpose, and direction to plan, design, develop and implement the changes defined by the tasks. It is the leader who sets the goals and priorities with total clarity. Likewise, it is up to the leader to define and maintain the standards and guiding principles by which the team operates.

Desired Outcomes

To align the organization and employees to support and sustain the vision.

Inputs

The defined pain points or the opportunities that triggered the commissioning of the change initiative.

Tools and Techniques

1. Communicate: Have honest discussions about the threats and opportunities, and give dynamic and convincing reasons to get people talking and thinking about how to change effectively.

2. Role modeling: Get involved in shaping the change through your actions.

3. Reward: Recognize and reward new behaviors, and people who help meet the targets.

Metrics

Mission success rate. This metric is calculated by the percentage of tasks in the track of work that had succeeded to meet their desired outcomes divided by the number of tasks.

Planning Considerations

The change champion of the People and Organization performance track does not need to hold the title of Human Resources Director or even be associated with that function. However, there are specific characteristics that each change champion should possess. These character traits are not as much about specific competencies of designing organizational structures, defining jobs or developing training, but rather they focus on the ability to lead employees to carry out their assigned tasks in order to complete the project's mission within a specific time frame, and achieving the desired outcomes. Listed in Appendix B is an evaluation assessment that is used to select and assess the change champion. This assessment evaluates twenty leadership characteristics needed for this role. The specific function of the People and Organization change champion is to address the human performance elements in the change initiative. Simply put, human performance describes the effectiveness of the actions people take to achieve their goals. A billing clerk, for instance, is considered to be performing at a high level if she is able to process many bills (high volume) with minimal errors (high quality). An individual using an airline ticketing kiosk is performing well if he is able to easily reserve an airline ticket, or check-in (ease of transaction).

Whatever the situation, whatever the audience, performance is measured in terms of the organization's business goals — the performance expectation. So, a billing clerk that perceives her goal to be reducing backlog — get through the stack of bills on her desk — is *not* necessarily performing at a high level, even if she has the shortest billing completion rate in the department. She is only at peak performance if her actions are in alignment with her true business objectives as defined by her organization — perhaps high volume *and* high quality. It is often the case that people are not aware of their true business goals; they have a misunderstanding of the external performance expectation.

Before proceeding, it's worth making a distinction between human performance and workforce performance. Workforce performance, as the name suggests, refers to the effectiveness of an organization's employees. Human performance is much broader. In analyzing human performance, we study a wide variety of people who impact an organization — workers, customers, subcontractors, suppliers, etc. Employment with the organization is not a requirement. Workforce performance, therefore, is a subset of human performance.

Validation of Outcomes
1. Were there frequent and honest discussions with the team members about the potential threats and an examination of the opportunities that should be taken?
2. Did the change champion describe the change vision in terms that could be easily understood and acted upon?
3. Was there an emotional commitment among the project team track that built a strong team coalition with support and guidance from the change champion?
4. Were obstacles identified and removed, allowing the project team to perform their task efficiently and effectively?
5. Were there defined goals and measures in place and clearly understood by project team members performing each key task?
6. Was the potential of the workforce fully utilized?

Core Values

Identify what is important to the organization.

This is performed at Level 1: Strategy.

Description

Core values are the very significant beliefs and principles that define the business. They are specialized standards set by a company regarding the method of its functioning, decision-making, problem-solving, and customer service. The primary benefit of core values is that they let employees and potential consumers know what the company is all about, and clarifies the identity of the company. A business may focus on providing the customer with a superior customer experience. As a result, systems, processes and job roles are all designed to support and align with this core value. However, threats to the business, such as an economic decline, may cause managers to seek cost-cutting measures and make decisions that detract from the core value. Seemingly insignificant changes throughout various parts of the business will have a cumulative effect that will erode the core values to both the employees and the customers, and will create longer lasting issues for the organization.

The core values of the organization never change and are those beliefs that differentiated the company, making it successful. Newer employees may not be aware, or even care, about these values. In a change initiative, these core values need to be identified and used as the standard to which all decisions for change are made. The question should be asked: If we automate this, or eliminate that, would it detract or enhance the core values? This initial task requires the identification, clarification and communication of the organization's core values.

Desired Outcomes

Every decision made within each track of work will align and support the core values of the organization.

Inputs
The documented core values of the organization.

Tools and Techniques
Checklists can be used to validate changes against the core values. An organizational culture assessment can be used to determine the behavioral norms and expectations that are currently present compared with the "ideal" behaviors that reflect alignment with the core values.

Metrics
Value alignment ratio. This metric calculates the ratio of decisions aligned to the core values against the total number of key decisions within each track of work.

Planning Considerations
One of the primary responsibilities of change leaders is to create and maintain the organizational characteristics that reward and encourage collective effort. Perhaps the most fundamental of these is organizational culture. The organization's culture is defined by the core values that reflect the basic principles that guide our interactions with every stakeholder of the organization. They also establish the boundaries of behavior for every employee. But within every large organization, behaviors can deviate from the norm. This departure is called a subculture because the group adapts some of the behaviors, but creates different actions that are unique to that group. Some groups can be completely counter to the behaviors of the other groups. This is an important concept to understand because what is valued and reinforced in one area may be punished in another. These specific differences are called causal factors and can create a barrier to change or enable the change to be sustained. It is important to recognize these behavioral differences early in the change initiative before they become risks.

One of the most recognizable examples of core values can be found within the U.S. Marine Corps. They have codified what they refer to as their "core values" of honor, courage and commitment. These attributes are the cornerstones of the Marine character, and are instilled in their daily life.

Core values are generally formulated by the founders of the organization. Although core values are beliefs, they are demonstrated in a number of ways. Whether the founders were aware of it or not, their individual values were brought forth in many ways: their ability to create and articulate the company's vision; their leadership style; their commitment to serving the customers; their selection and placement of people into specific roles; their structure of the organization; and their enforcement of policies to maintain control, are just a few examples.

Unfortunately, it is all too common for companies to profess allegiance to their core values while behaving in utter disregard of them. In situations such as this, the change leadership should agree to a set of principles or standards on which to base their decisions.

Validation of Outcomes

1. Core values have been identified, understood and agreed upon to use as the standard to evaluate the key decisions within the change initiative.
2. A process is designed to efficiently and effectively evaluate decisions and propose recommendations and alternatives to ensure alignment to the core values.
3. The organization's culture (behavioral norms and expectations) are aligned to the core values.
4. Employees know what the core values are and what they mean.
5. Change champions demonstrate the core values in leading the change.

Change Vision

Describe how the organization will look in the future

This is performed at Level 1: Strategy.

Description

A vision for change creates a picture of the future that inspires people to work to make it come true. Once the problem is identified and analyzed, there probably will be many great ideas and solutions that leaders will embrace. A clear vision for change will help focus and direct a formulation of a solution that will not only meet the immediate concerns of employees, but will position the organization to meet the needs of the future.

A vision is a clearly defined goal affecting all employees. When the vision is stated in realistic, achievable, and measurable terms, the easier it will be for employees to accomplish. A vision answers the question "why" something needs to be accomplished by relating it to the core values and beliefs of others.

A great change vision statement is something that is easy for a broad range of people to understand — from the administrative assistant to the most senior executive. The change vision should be written down so that other change leaders understand and communicate a consistent message. Generally, the change vision statement is no longer than a half page, which makes it easy to communicate in a way that people will "get it" and buy into the change.

What the change champion will need to do is:
- Determine the values central to the change initiative.
- Develop a short summary that clearly describes the future of the organization.

33

- Ensure the vision is shared by all senior leaders and that the message is consistent.
- Create a strategy to execute that vision.
- Continually restate the vision in terms others clearly understand.

Desired Outcomes

To have any member of the project team state the vision and be able to articulate what it means to the organization and personally to the employees.

Inputs

The problem statement or opportunity; the organization's core values; and the scope of the initiative.

Tools and Techniques

1. Use a collaborative work session with senior leaders, change champions and key stakeholders to develop the vision for change.
2. Use the checklist to clarify and determine if the vision statement meets the requirements.
3. Communicate the vision often, then "walk the talk."

Metrics

Vision alignment rate: The percent of changes implemented over time.

Planning Considerations

Communicating the vision is essential to the success of the change initiative. The leaders of the change initiative need to use every means at their disposal to constantly communicate the new vision and key strategies that support the vision. This goes beyond the "special announcement" meetings, and will involve frequent and informal face-to-face contact with the project team and the stakeholders. These meetings should be conducted by the senior leadership to reinsure employees of their involvement and commitment. E-mail is not the appropriate communication vehicle, except in support of prior face-to-face meetings. But it goes further than talking about the change, the leadership team needs to visibly "walk the talk" and at all times be available and accessible to the employees to answer their questions and elevate their fears by being open and honest.

Think of the communication around the change vision as a campaign. The vision of the future should be clear in everybody's mind as to how the organization will look, feel and operate. The use of multiple communication vehicles at key points along the journey can be very effective. These may include informal discussions and group meetings with senior leaders; short videos, demonstrations, graphics and posters; e-mail blasts, websites and memos.

Validation of Outcomes
1. Does your vision describe what an activity or group might look like in the future?
2. For customers who are satisfied today, will the picture of the future painted in the vision keep them satisfied?
3. For customers who are not entirely happy today, will this make them happier?
4. For people who don't buy from you now, will this attract them?
5. In a few years, will you be doing a better job than the competition of offering products and services that serve real customer needs?
6. Will this keep stakeholders satisfied?
7. If stakeholders are not entirely happy today, will this improve matters?
8. If employees are satisfied today, will this keep them happy?
9. If employees are disgruntled, will this help capture their minds and hearts?
10. If you are successful with this change, will you be able to offer better employment opportunities than other companies with whom you compete in the labor market?
11. Does your vision set out stretch goals that are, nevertheless, achievable with great effort?
12. Does the vision statement provide a compelling story to all target audiences?

13. Does the vision statement provide clear focus and direction at every level?
14. Is the vision statement easy to communicate (thirty-second description)?
15. Does the vision provide flexibility to key target groups?
16. Does the vision provide a clear picture of the future?
17. Is the vision doable in the time frame allotted?
18. Is your vision grounded in a clear rational understanding of the business operation?
19. Does your vision describe not just where you are going, but also how you will get there?
20. Is your vision vague enough to allow individual initiative and flexibility in light of changing conditions?
21. Is your vision focused and clear enough to provide guidance in decision-making?
22. Is your vision ambitious enough to force people out of their comfort zone?
23. Does your vision take advantage of fundamental trends in your industry?
24. Can your vision be easily communicated by others?
25. Does your vision have meaning to all of the target audiences at every level?
26. Does your vision have moral power behind it (makes no attempt to exploit anyone)?

Guiding Principles

The ideology that will guide the change

This is performed at Level 1: Strategy.

Description

Once the core values of the organization have been identified, and the change vision has been developed, the next step is to define how the change vision will be executed. Guiding principles are the standards which the project team will follow to transition the current state of the organization to a new way of behaving and interacting with customers and suppliers. It also serves as a personal code of conduct that leads, shows the way and directs the movements of your project. A set of guiding principles adds value and makes the project progress faster only if the project team members do the things this definition implies.

Change can be very emotional as well as political. To ensure success, the morals, values and beliefs to deal with individuals have to be defined and commonly agreed to by all. The core values describe "why" we are doing the change; the change vision describes "how" the change will provide value; and the guiding principles describe "what" the project team will do to smoothly transition the organization. Communicating the guiding principles is equally important as the vision statement.

Desired Outcomes

To have the changes implemented on time, using the defined standards that will support and guide the people impacted by the change.

Inputs

The vision statement and the core values.

Tools and Techniques

1. Use a collaborative work session with senior leaders, change champions and key stakeholders to develop the guiding

principles. This will build support and buy-in among senior leaders.

2. Communicate the guiding principles as part of the overall change plan.

3. Provide examples and demonstrate the value of the guiding principles.

Metrics

Guiding principle acceptance rate — the acceptance of the change activity over a defined time.

Planning Considerations

Defining your beliefs and guiding principles is important for implementing a change initiative. If you don't define your beliefs, others associated with the project, or impacted by the project, will do it for you. By defining what's important to achieve success and taking ownership of those standards, you are setting up a system that will guide your project team through the pain and disruption that is often accompanied by large-scale change. Defining the guiding principles is similar to defining the core values. It is not enough that one leader has described the values and principles that will guide the change initiative. Other leaders need to understand and support these beliefs in the day-to-day management of the project. To gain a common understanding, it is recommended to use a collaborative work session where the project team members can identify the policies, rules and procedures in the project, which either:

- have a negative impact on morale;
- are unnecessary obstacles in the way of getting the change implemented quickly, with minimal disruption, and maintaining consistent quality; or
- eliminate or change those who are irrational and don't support the business to achieve its goals.

Guiding principles can either be expressed by using a word followed by a short explanation or in bullet points. The format does not matter as long as the project team understands and applies these principles to guide the decisions to ensure success. Following are some actual examples:

Trust in the Group Process — Collaborative group members agree to have trust in the group process; that the steps they are working on together represent forward progress; and the right outcomes will result from trusting the process, even if individuals don't always agree.

Openness — Collaborative group members agree to remain open to other points of view, all group members, the group process and its outcomes.

- "Under promise, over deliver"
- "We always err on the side of the customer"
- "We're honest in our dealings with each other and the public"
- "We take immediate responsibility for our actions, both personally and as a company"

Validation of Outcomes
1. Each member of the project team knows and understands the guiding principles.
2. Decisions are based upon the principles and standards that have been established.
3. The leadership team openly supports these principles through their talk and actions.
4. The project team operates more efficiently, and tasks are completed on schedule.
5. The project team members and key stakeholders are satisfied and trust in the change.

Goal Setting

Establish clear goals for the change initiative.

This is performed at Level 2: Tactical.

Description

The strategy activities have created the vision and the overall plan to achieve the objective. Goal setting is the first tactical task to be performed. Goal setting activities help to plan the relevant tasks that need to be performed to ensure that the change goal can be attained within a specific time frame. The S.M.A.R.T. method assumes the goals that are set are: **S**pecific, **M**easurable, **A**ttainable, **R**ealistic and **T**ime Bound. Specifics help us to focus our efforts and clearly define what we are going to do. If you can't measure it, you can't manage it. In the broadest sense, the whole goal statement is a measure for the project; if the goal is accomplished, there is a success. However, there are usually several short-term or small measurements that can be built into the goal. Once the goal has been defined, there must be adequate resources and competencies to obtain the goal within the define time frame. Realistic is not a synonym for "easy." Realistic, in this case, means "doable." The project team has all of the resources at hand and the capabilities to complete the tasks assigned. Putting an end point on the task gives the project team a clear target to work towards. If you don't set a time and ability to track the progress, then the commitment will be too vague and not create the sense of urgency to complete the task.

Desired Outcomes

To have specific, measureable goals, that are attainable and realistic, with specific time frames that can be tracked successfully to complete and support the project.

Inputs

A well-defined strategic plan, including a clear vision of the future.

Tools and Techniques

- Use the S.M.A.R.T. technique to define the goals.
- Develop goals within a collaborative environment. Goal setting is a shared process so the project team will be more committed to achieving the objectives. You will be surprised what new possibilities your project team members come up with when you ask for their help.

Metrics

Goal completion ratio: This metric calculates the ratio of goals achieved against the total number of goals attempted.

Planning Considerations

Incremental improvements start with a known standard or level of performance where adjustments in staffing levels, individual performance and training can improve operational performance targets. Providing incentives or increasing morale also aids to achieve the goals. However, in a transformational change, there may not be the usual means to establish goals. These new targets are developed from the change vision and will be further defined as the project develops new capabilities. Using the change vision statement, specific requirements are defined. These requirements may be new key performance indicators such as a level of quality, or number of defects. They also could be new service levels or the turnaround time of a product, or the overall volume delivered. In the service industry, it could relate to the processing speed, or the number of calls handled. Each of these examples has specific requirements that can be measurable. It is not enough just to measure the outcome because the number will not have a meaning unless it is in relation to another variable. When two variables are identified, it becomes a metric. Metrics will be discussed in greater detail in the next activity. The goal must be attainable; this can be subjective especially if the goal has never been attempted. However, attainability comes from knowing your capabilities (people, processes, technologies and information).

Being relevant means that the goal is fulfilling the needs of your customer and the organization's broader goals, such as to make a profit, sustain the community or satisfy the shareholders. Finally, the goal must be attainable within the specified time requirements of the change initiative and operational objective. Use the S.M.A.R.T. method when evaluating all change initiative goals.

Chart your progress. The most satisfying part of goal setting is observing successful achievement of short-term goals and checking off tasks from the master list. A regular progress report identifies whether you are on the right course. Evaluate if the goals are being achieved. Early assessment and evaluation of each goal is helpful to identify risks or barriers. The leadership team should make adjustments as needed to ensure each short- and long-term goal is achievable.

Validation of Outcomes
1. Avoid goals that are overambitious or you may risk company reputation and violate ethical standards.
2. Don't mentally beat up your project team members if they fail at meeting one of the goals, or you might lose their support.
3. Too many unrealistic goals could direct employees to have less confidence in your ability to lead.
4. Regularly measure short- and long-term goals to ensure progress is being made.
5. Identify and evaluate potential risks and assumptions that may block goal attainment.

Performance Metrics (Operational)

Identify the key metrics that will measure the change.

This is performed at Level 2: Tactical.

Description

A performance metric is a standard in which two measurements are compared and generally reported as a ratio or percentage. There may be a variety of performance indicators to measure and compare; however, there are only a few critical measures called key metrics that can be used to assess the effectiveness of the change initiative. Metrics are also used to measure the health of the project and consist of the measuring of six criteria: time, cost, resources, scope, quality and actions. Metrics are also referred to as key performance indicators (KPI) or key success indicators (KSI). However, they are somewhat different. Key or critical success factors are areas that differentiate the organization from others and, therefore, are vital to the success of the organization. Once the critical areas have been identified, the KPIs identify the specific areas to be monitored. The metric, therefore, is a comparison between the specific variables. Performance measures are often used in finance to determine the operational efficiency of the business. Performance metrics for the change initiative are unique for each initiative because they are based upon the defined outcomes.

Desired Outcomes

Selecting and using the metrics that are key to the success of the change initiative ensure that the activities are effective and move the organization in the right direction to meet the vision.

Inputs

The vision of the future state supported by the guiding principles. Project inputs include an understanding of the scope of the change, the timeframes in which the change needs to take place, the cost, resources, and level of quality expected.

Tools and Techniques

1. Educate project leaders and key stakeholders on the importance of performance measurement and the meaning of metrics, critical success factors and key performance indicators.
2. Have the leadership identify those activities that differentiate the business and make them unique. There should not be more than four critical success factors identified making it easier to monitor the changes. Ensure the leadership is in agreement.
3. Identify the key performance indicators that directly impact your change initiative that will need to be monitored.
4. Select the appropriate metric and measurement techniques for specific tasks or operations within the project.
5. Establish a schedule to routinely monitor the changes and to take appropriate action.

Metrics

There are no metrics used to measure the effectiveness of the metrics chosen for the project

Planning Considerations

Many people believe that metrics and measures are interchangeable, that they have the same meaning. However, the simple definition of a metric is the standard, and the measure is the act. We could say we have earned $5,000.00, and that, in effect, is the measure. However, the amount offers no relevance and, consequently, it does not have significant meaning unless it is compared with another variable. The dollar amount is only a data point, and we cannot say if that is a lot or a little amount of money. That is why we need to establish a reference point.

Let us label our metric as Human Capital ROI (Return on Investment). The description of this metric is defined as profit an organization generates for each dollar invested in a regular employee's pay and benefits after operating expenses are removed. The metric is expressed as a ratio and as a result, will provide significance to the overall investment made to an employee's total compensation. The two measures associated with this metric are the employee base pay, and the organization's profit. The metric determines the profitability for every dollar that is invested in their employees.

There are many different ways that an organization can define a metric. Metrics are used throughout the organization and can provide some valuable information. Almost every activity that is defined in this book has a metric which can determine if the activity is producing the desired result. However, an organization can get lost in the use of metrics. For this reason, select only those metrics that are determined to be useful at that particular time.

Validation of Outcomes
1. The metric is defined in terms of two measurable variables.
2. The measures used within the metric are objectively measureable.
3. The metric focus on effectiveness and/or efficiency of the system being measured.
4. The metric allows for meaningful trend or statistical analysis.
5. The metric being mutually agreed upon by the business leaders.
6. Those who are responsible for the performance being measured are fully involved in the development of this metric.
7. A key metric has been identified for this initiative and track of work.

Inter-unit Coordination

Develop collaboration between business units and departments.

This is performed at Level 2: Tactical.

Description

The exchange of information and the coordination of work tasks are essential to the success of an organization. Many leaders believe that new technological innovations will revolutionize their organizations through automation of workflow, increased communication from mobile applications, and improved decision-making through enhanced reporting, dashboards and analytic tools. They fervently believe that new products and processes will automatically enhance jobs, increase productivity and make their businesses more competitive in global markets. Yet, in order for a new technology to have revolutionary impact, it has to be aligned to the operational culture, the accepted business practices, the defined processes, and the structure of the organization. Without addressing the relationships, the ability for each work group, department and business unit to be effective and productive will be hampered. In addition, valuable knowledge within the organization is too often "locked-in" within one unit, often called tribal knowledge. The knowledge-sharing enablers such as trust, respect, communication style and quality, and empowerment are some of the behaviors that are needed to increase inter-unit coordination.

Desired Outcomes

Create an adaptive and constructive culture. This type of culture values good leadership by encouraging teamwork at the top, while minimizing layers of bureaucracy, as well as counterproductive interdependencies. Employees are encouraged to interact with people and approach tasks in ways that help them meet their higher-order satisfaction needs.

Inputs

Understanding of the organization's core values dictates the "ideal" culture.

Tools and Techniques

1. Identify the current behaviors of each department or business unit. This could be performed using an assessment tool and interviews.
2. Identify the desired behaviors based upon the core values of the organization.
3. Identify the gaps between each department or business units against the behaviors supported by the core values. Identify the causal factors and barriers to change.
4. Develop a gap closure plan to align the organization to create an adaptive and constructive culture by leveraging the change in the causal factors.

Metrics

Organizational cultural gap: The difference between the current state culture and the ideal culture based upon the organization's core values.

Planning Considerations

Inter-unit coordination is about creating an environment where information is shared and work is transitioned smoothly and effectively across the organization, starting from the supplier entry point to providing the customer with the product or service, meeting their expectations of quality, and providing value to both the customer and the business. To achieve this standard, there needs to be coordination, collaboration and integration: streamlined business processes, defined by the knowledge, enhanced by the technology, and enabled by the people and organization to achieve desired outcomes.

An operational culture that supports adaptive and constructive behaviors is what makes inter-unit coordination uniquely effective. It is the set of values, principles, norms, policies and signs manifested by its employees in their day-to-day operations that should be taken into account as the ground rules for their work. However, as the organization matures, bureaucratic systems and procedures take over creating levels of hierarchy and control. Work can then become complex and hard to manage. Challenges and differing leadership styles within business units and departments can shift the culture, differentiating it from other areas and creating barriers. There are many causal factors that influence and define behaviors. Identifying the differences between the business units and departments, then aligning them to one common pattern of behavior defined by the organization's core values will greatly improve inter-unit coordination.

Barriers can develop between units, departments or work groups when the people in these groups become overly protective of their activities and resist any outside influence. They may have their own time schedules to complete their tasks or wish to set priorities that may differ from other units. The leader of these units may know their capabilities and limitations and might fear outside influence and will challenge their authority or expose a weakness. The fears of these leaders could be real or imagined. Exposing a weakness in the manager's ability to lead or the unit's ability to perform can be detrimental on an individual, unit and organizational level. This is why an organizational culture that supports individuals, as well as accomplishing tasks to desired performance levels, is encouraged.

Barriers do not have to be individual deficiencies. Business processes may be broken or inefficient. Software applications and their associated infrastructures may perform at less than desirable levels, or information needed to perform tasks may be incomplete, outdated or inaccessible. In many cases, it is a combination of all of these factors which will create barriers or other restrictions thus limiting the coordination of activities across the organization.

There are several useful assessment tools to identify and categorize these causal factors which can be used for inter-unit coordination. However, assessments are not always practical. Identifying and assessing the causal factors through interviews and discussion groups can also determine less subtle differences. Some of the more common traits may include: selection and placement practices, communication styles, rewards and punishments, training and development, organizational structure, job design, defined business processes, and leadership and managerial styles.

Validation of Outcomes

1. Project leaders and key stakeholders know and understand both the positive and negative effects of inter-unit coordination.
2. Barriers that block or limit inter-unit coordination between business units and departments are removed, allowing information and work to flow efficiently through the organization.
3. Aligning the organization's culture to create adaptive and constructive behaviors is part of the change initiative and actively supported.
4. Performance metrics are used to measure the change in behavior throughout the transformation.
5. Business processes and technical capabilities are evaluated and aligned to support the culture.

Organizational Structure

Examine how employees work together within a team environment.

This is performed at Level 3: Operational.

Description

An organization is composed of many parts. For the organization to be effective, it is essential that each part be in good working condition. Each part must fit and work conjointly with other parts for the total organization to perform optimally. In an organization recognized for excellence, those parts are aligned so the whole is actually more effective than the sum of the parts.

In an organization, a number of activities are performed. These activities are required to be coordinated. Organization structure is designed for division of tasks, grouping of activities, and coordinating and controlling the tasks of the organization. A detailed study of all components and dimensions of organizational structure is required for the creation of an efficient and stable structure. A well-designed organizational structure facilitates the smooth functioning of the organization.

There are two basic models of organizational structure: one founded on the concept of management, and one founded on the concept of leadership. The former operates from the foundational belief that one controls results by controlling resources. The latter operates from a foundational belief that by giving up control of resources it is possible to get greater control over results. To create an effective and efficient organization, I believe that leaders create the vision and guide the change, and are effective by removing barriers and allowing employees the freedom to make decisions. The role of management is to manage the process, not the people.

Desired Outcomes

The organization is designed to achieve effective and efficient outcomes it intends to produce, giving employees the autonomy to make decisions.

- Structures and behaviors are aligned with business needs.
- Disruption to business is minimized, which reduces operational risk.
- Employee morale is sustained, which maintains productivity.
- The right employees and talents are retained.
- Employees' objectives and rewards are aligned to business goals.

Inputs

The core values and guiding principles establish the framework in which employees will operate. An organizational culture assessment will identify the causal factors that exist within the structure. The inter-unit coordination will ensure that information and activities are performed to defined standards.

Tools and Techniques

In the context of the change initiative, the activities should focus on these key elements:

1. Operational strategic intent
2. Performance targets
3. Business capabilities (staffing levels, technology, working environment)
4. Defined business processes
5. Dependencies
6. Working relationships (such as high-performing teams)

Metrics

Revenue factor: The amount of revenue an organization generates divided by each regular full-time equivalency (FTE).

Management ratio: The number of regular headcount employees each manager and executive supports divided by the total headcount (also known as the span of control).

Planning Considerations

The organization has to be both effective and efficient to be successful. Organizational effectiveness is a measure of the extent to which an organization realizes its goals. Organizational efficiency refers to the amount of resources an organization uses in order to produce a unit of output. Efficiency and effectiveness are highly dependent on the ability of the organization to adjust itself to rapid changes in its environment, resources or technology.

The organization needs to be assessed on how job tasks are formally divided, grouped and coordinated. To achieve organizational effectiveness, six elements need to be addressed while designing organizational structure. These are work specialization, departmentalization, chain of command, span of control, centralization and decentralization, and formalization of reporting relationships.

Validation of Outcomes

1. Is there a high level of employee satisfaction within the organization?
2. Are the customers and suppliers (internal and external) satisfied with the organization?
3. Does the organizational unit (department, business unit) provide measurable value?
4. Is the organization growing in terms of profit, revenue, number of products, expansion into new locations, line of products, etc.?
5. Is the organization productive, i.e., creating goods and services of high value at minimum cost?

Job/Position Design

Create autonomy, significance, variety and influence.

This is performed at Level 3: Operational.

Description

Within traditional organizations each job and position is well-defined and documented. Essentially, every job has a specific role and purpose. This can lead to a highly structured and complex work environment. To complete a complex activity, there needs to be a division of labor which involves breaking the activity into a number of simpler tasks and assigning these tasks to specialists who generally perform only their assigned duties. This process works effectively, especially in highly regulated work environments. However, when change is introduced, it is difficult for the organization to readily adapt.

In a large-scale change initiative, job requirements could drastically change. With the automation of administrative tasks by new software, applications replaced the tasks that were once done manually. The advent of cloud computing allows for greater mobility, resulting in greater flexibility in scheduling work and using the virtual office to coordinate work over a greater geographic area. These changes will rearrange or replace the way in which work groups function, teams operate and the division of labor.

Desired Outcomes

Create a work environment which satisfies the technical and organizational requirements as well as the social and personal requirements of the jobholder.

Inputs

The business policies and compliance rules, the high-level business requirements, the critical processes, the organizational structure and the performance levels.

Tools and Techniques
- Use employee satisfaction surveys to determine the level of fulfillment
- Perform exit interviews to identify reoccurring themes or issues
- Build team unity and collaboration in daily job duties

Metrics
Voluntary separation rate: The percentage of regular employee headcount who voluntarily left the organization over a specified time frame.

Planning Considerations
There are many aspects of job design that need to be evaluated during a large-scale transformation effort. The leadership team should focus on creating an organization that is nimble, adapting to internal and external changes without creating disruption of service. I have identified four aspects of the job design that need to be considered.

Work Organization
- Rearranging or replacing work (e.g., automating, teaming, work groups, division of labor)
- Giving the worker additional responsibilities/tasks (job enlargement)
- Job rotation

Job Structuring
- Giving responsibility for different types/levels of work (job enrichment)
- Granting control over work (autonomy)
- Self-organization (time/process management)

Location/Scheduling
- Telecommuting (part or full off-site work)
- Alternative scheduling (4 four-day work week, flextime, job sharing, etc.)
- Virtual office/virtual organization

Significant Job Characteristics

Variety	• Removal of repetitiveness
	• Skill variety
Autonomy	• Removal of no choice of tools or methods
	• Removal of mechanical pacing
	• Ability to make decisions
Use of Capacities	• Removal of minimal skill requirements
	• Removal of surface mental attention
	• Creation of learning time
	• Making the job challenging
Progress/ Career Path	• Recognize achievements
	• Identify opportunities for advancement
	• Support growth in competence
	• Promote continuous learning
	• Create a desirable future
Intrinsically Meaningful Work	• Remove minute subdivision of processes
	• Create task identity to the whole product
Socially Meaningful Work	• Make tasks significant
	• Balance work and social life
Interaction	• Create interaction opportunities
	• Provide social support and recognition
Knowledge of Results	• Provide recognition of work performed
	• Give feedback
Responsibility	• Make employees accountable
	• Provide choices over methods and tools

Validation of Outcomes

Provide proof of job design changes as outlined above that will support the change vision in conjunction with the capabilities.

Role Competencies

Define new competencies for each role.

This is performed at Level 3: Operational.

Description

A job represents a specific set of tasks, duties and responsibilities that are performed within an organization. These elements are normally documented, and generally measured. Job classes or families can be used to define the degree of performance or responsibility that is required at that particular level. An entry level project manager-1 job may be responsible for tracking and reporting tasks completed, where a project manager-3 may be required to plan and coordinate tasks across multiple streams of work. There are a set of requirements that are common at each level of the job; the difference is the level at which they are performed and new tasks based on the level of responsibility.

A position on the other hand is a unique role within an organization that is defined by the job, but requires an additional unique set of competencies. In my example; the marketing department and information systems department both need a project manager-2. Although the job of project manager is the same, requiring project skills at a specific performance level, the position will require department specific competencies in order to function effectively in that role.

Competencies are defined as knowledge, skills, abilities and behaviors needed for the role. Knowledge competencies may be general awareness to specific information which may be gained through formal education or certification. Skills are tasks that are gained through training and experience. Abilities define the degree in which the skill is performed, the degree of intelligence or the competence. Behaviors define the particular way a response to a situation is performed, such as making decisions or leadership abilities.

Desired Outcomes

All positions within the scope of the change initiative are defined including the reporting relationships.

Inputs

Defined jobs and positions, organizational structure, and processes.

Tools and Techniques

- Competency model
- Gather the behaviors and knowledge for each role/position
- Define a scale for each competency
- Gap analysis and gap closure

Metrics

Competency compliance: The ability to meet defined operational performance levels by measuring the individual compliance against operational performance.

Planning Considerations

During a change initiative, new technologies and changes in business processes can often change job competencies which may completely change the job role, staffing levels or reporting relationships. Administrative tasks may be automated by the technology and create a shift in competencies. The competency of sorting, filing and data entry would no longer be required of that role. The new competency may now require the analysis of information to solve problems and make decisions. The knowledge level has shifted from knowing the required data and the order in which it needs to be collected and entered towards understanding what the information represents and the relative importance to the business. The new behaviors that will be required demonstrate leadership skills by interacting with others to collaboratively problem-solve and make informed decisions. The administrative task may have once required several people to accomplish, and managers performed the analysis. Now fewer people are required to perform the analysis. The role may now report their findings and interact with other roles.

When business processes are mapped and documented, specific activities, tasks and work steps are identified in the work stream. The performance metrics assist in assessing the capability level in which the competency is performed. When creating high-performance teams, the organizational structure is relatively flat. Role competencies in a team environment tend to be broader than within a highly structured, vertical organization.

As new technologies enhance the business process, new competencies are needed to support the change. The dynamics of the team will change by the ability to exchange information and increase visibility to other team member's work. As the work group matures into a high-performing team, the traditional roles with their defined competencies will evolve and will be shared equally among team members, thereby creating the knowledge worker.

It is important to remember that these competencies relate to the role and not the candidate or employee fulfilling the role. The individual's competencies will be measured against the role competencies. A gap analysis should be performed to determine the competency gap between the job role and the candidate filling the role. A gap closure plan will describe the most appropriate method to close the competency gap. This may range from on-the-job guidance to selecting candidates more suitable to fill the position.

Validation of Outcomes
1. Job competencies: Knowledge, skills, abilities and behaviors are defined.
2. Position competencies are defined.
3. Competencies are measurable and documented.
4. Role competencies are used in recruitment and selection.
5. Role competencies are derived from business processes.

Job Fit and Selection

Select employees that fit to the newly defined role.

This is performed at Level 4: Functional.

Description

Think about your best employees. Not only does he/she do the job well, he/she is highly motivated, contributing to the culture and morale of the company. What would it mean to your organization if you could determine a strong job fit during the selection process? It starts with understanding the competency requirements of the job role, and matching those competencies and behaviors to the candidate to ensure the best fit. Having the right people in the right jobs will result in strong employee retention, increased productivity and performance, and higher morale, all of which are critical to the future and bottom-line success of your business.

Job fit is the process of matching the competencies and characteristics of an individual to the organization, the department and the position. It is not enough for a candidate just to have the skills and the years of experience to adequately perform the tasks to acceptable performance levels, but also to align and demonstrate the core values of the organization with the candidate.

Desired Outcomes

Have alignment of candidates to the job roles within the scope of the change initiative.

Inputs

The job role competencies defined, and the job designed to fit within the organizational structure. Business rules, policies and procedures defined to provide guidance, and the technology and tools developed to support the job.

Tools and Techniques

1. All job roles and positions that are within the scope of a major change initiative should be evaluated to determine the type and amount of change.
2. An approved transition plan should be in place prior to any role or position being evaluated.
3. Use behavioral interviewing to determine the alignment of individual characteristics with the organization's core values, culture and behaviors defined in the position.
4. Psychometric testing is useful to measure the knowledge, skills, abilities, attitudes, personality traits and educational measurement for a job fit.

Metrics

1. The voluntary separation ratio: The ratio of regular employee headcount that voluntarily left the organization over a given period of time.
2. The involuntary separation ratio: The ratio of regular employee headcount that involuntarily left the organization over a given period of time.

Planning Considerations

I do not support using job descriptions to select candidates for a number of reasons. My primary reason is that job descriptions define tasks, but can limit the capabilities of individuals in their roles. Written job descriptions set boundaries on what can or cannot be performed. However, this works well in traditional and bureaucratic organizations where every role has a very specific purpose, scope and responsibilities. Nevertheless, this level of staffing can become quite costly when economic conditions are weak. To respond quickly to change, organizations prefer to create roles that are broadly defined, working in a team environment. When supporting high-performing teams, members are cross-trained and cross-functional. They often function as self-directed teams responding to broad, but not specific directives. Therefore, job descriptions cannot adequately define or capture the leadership qualities, values, and beliefs that are characteristic of these roles. Next, job descriptions are written for current requirements and not those that will continually evolve.

Many organizations are using behavioral-based interviewing to determine job fit. The premise behind behavioral interviewing is that the most accurate predictor of future performance is past performance in similar situations. Behavioral interviewing, in fact, is said to be fifty-five percent predictive of future on-the-job behavior, while traditional interviewing is only ten percent predictive. Traditional interview questions ask you general questions such as: "Tell me about yourself." The process of behavioral interviewing is much more probing and works very differently. Behavioral-based interviewing is touted as providing a more objective set of facts to make employment decisions than the traditional interviewing method.

In addition to behavioral-based interviewing, some organizations use psychometric testing. A psychometric instrument is capable of providing a complete job-fit analysis by comparing the job role or position-required competencies against selected candidates to determine best fit. In addition to pre-employment screening, they can be used for internal advancement, coaching and counseling, training and development, and succession planning.

Validation of Outcomes
1. An approved transition and development plan has been created.
2. All individuals filling roles directly impacted by the change initiative have been assessed to determine if they still have the right competencies to fulfill the new requirements.
3. A skills development program is in place for those who meet the role competency requirements but are not proficient in specific skills.

Individual Competencies

Measure and develop individual competencies for the role / position.

This is performed at Level 4: Functional.

Description

Part of the transformation initiative is to recognize and develop an environment for continuous learning to more readily identify and adapt to the changes within the organization. Once an individual is in a role does not mean that there is no longer a need to learn. Changes within the organization, the process, the work group and the job role are continually changing. Learning should not be confused with training. Training is something an organization provides for their employees that focuses on the event, whereas learning puts the emphasis on the learner to obtain and apply the new information. By allowing employees to be part of their development and providing the tools for learning, the environment will be formed.

Measurement of individual learning is defined by the job performance. Research shows that while ninety-five percent of organizations measure the degree to which employees like the training, sixty-three percent fail to measure whether or not employees learned anything applicable to their job, and a shocking ninety-seven percent fail to measure whether the learning actually impacted job performance. Performance metrics and measures are used to provide continuous feedback on the job performance.

Peter Drucker predicted that the major changes in business would be brought about by information sharing. He stated that "knowledge has become the central, key resource that knows no geography." He went on to state that the largest working group will become what he termed "knowledge workers."

Desired Outcomes

An environment for learning is created by active employee participation, defined performance metrics and measures, and providing the necessary tools for learning.

Inputs

Job fit requirements and the gap to the role competencies.

Tools and Techniques

- Incorporate principles of adult learning. This includes creating an environment that motivates and rewards individual learning.
- Provide access to training aids, guides, application access, training data bases and other support material.

Metrics

Training cost factor: The average amount spent on training for each regular employee receiving training.

Planning Considerations

In today's "high-performance organizations," workers must be prepared for continuous on-the-job learning and development. Given the generational differences, variety of experiences, and diverse cultures of the working population, it is understandable that adult education practices must move beyond the traditional model of teachers as purveyors of knowledge and learners as passive recipients. Methods and techniques that draw upon workers' previous experiences, link concepts and practices, and encourage reflection and the transfer of knowledge from one situation to another are vital to the learning process. Listed below are new ways to learn at work.

Action learning is a systematic process through which individuals learn by doing. It is based on the premise that learning requires action, and action requires learning. It engages individuals in just-in-time learning by providing opportunities for them to develop knowledge and understanding, at the appropriate time, based on immediate-felt needs.

Situational learning is another workplace learning approach. In this approach, knowledge and skills are taught in contexts that reflect how the knowledge will be used in real-life situations. This strategy is based on the premise that knowledge is not independent, but fundamentally situated, being, in part, a product of the activity, context and culture in which it is developed.

Incidental learning is defined as an unplanned action, the intent of which task accomplishment increases particular knowledge or skills. Incidental learning, then, includes such things as learning from mistakes, learning by doing, learning through networking, and learning from a series of interpersonal experiments. Incidental learning is unintentional and unexamined. It is not based on reflection; thus the learning is embedded in the learner's actions.

Validation of Outcomes
1. The work environment supports and encourages learning at all levels where it can be recognized and rewarded.
2. Performance metrics and measures continually monitor the result of the employee learning where adjustments can be made.
3. Learning value is documented in the knowledge base and learning management system (LMS).
4. Training/job aids, training data bases, access to software applications and other support materials are developed and made available.

Rewards and Recognition

Identify and implement a system that promotes new behaviors that align with the organizational change.

This is performed at Level 4: Functional.

Description

Workforce recognition and rewards are developed to motivate employees and maintain or increase their motivation and satisfaction. Recognition is essential in times of change. Behaviors that reinforce the new way to perform business operations needs to be encouraged and supported. It may be difficult to break old habits and act in a way that feels uncomfortable. It is the responsibility of the change champion and other leaders to publically recognize the efforts of an individual or group that is making a decision, interacting with customers, or performing a task that is consistent with the vision for change. Rewards are used at various milestones in the project when a visible effort has been made to operate the "new" way. It may be difficult for the organization to transition and require recognition of small accomplishments. At this point, old behaviors should not be punished, rather ignored.

Team rewards are understood as important motivators to accomplish organizational objectives. Four factors need to be considered in establishing team-based rewards: the stages of a team life cycle; reward and recognition categories; the type of teams; and the culture of the team and organization.

Specific reward tools should be identified which can be used for individual or team incentives. Greater emphasis is placed on team rewards rather than individual rewards. The reason to place less emphasis on an individual is not to promote superstar personalities, but rather promote team collaboration. Comprehensive metrics are identified and used to determine the most appropriate tool at a specific stage in a team's life cycle to measure their level of performance. A cost-benefit analysis should be performed to determine the overall value. An evaluation of team reward systems is then considered.

Desired Outcomes
To promote and reinforce change and employee satisfaction.

Inputs
Well-communicated change vision and goals, along with an understanding of the competencies, roles and structure in which to operate.

Tools and Techniques
- Identify the critical success factors to base recognition and rewards.
- The best rewards are often the ones that are more personal in nature.
- The best recognition is timely and meaningful.
- Find out what works in their organizations and what their employees want from a rewards and recognition program.

Metrics
Rate of change ratio: Measure the compliance to change divided by the total time allotted for the change.

Planning Considerations
Although reward and recognition are often used interchangeably, they should be considered separately. Employee reward systems refer to programs set up by the organization to reward performance and motivate employees on individual and/or group levels. They are normally considered separate from salary, but may be monetary in nature or otherwise have a cost associated with them.

Recognition is a powerful tool and, when used correctly, can achieve commanding results. Employee recognition is the timely, informal or formal, acknowledgment of a person's or team's behavior, effort or business result that supports the organization's goals and values, which has clearly exceeded normal expectations.

However, when used inappropriately, the recognition can completely lose its value and credibility among employees. Recognition, whether given to an individual or group, must be done in public.

Appreciation is a fundamental human need. Employees respond to appreciation expressed through recognition of good work because it confirms that their work is valued. When employees' work is valued, satisfaction and productivity rises, and they are motivated to maintain or improve their good work.

During the change initiative, employees may feel uncertain if their actions are correct and if their decisions are appropriate in the new environment. That is why praise and recognition are essential during a change initiative in order to promote the new behaviors. Employees want to know that their contribution to the change effort is valued. Everyone feels the need to be recognized as an individual or member of a group and to feel a sense of achievement for work well done, or even for a valiant effort.

Validation of Outcomes
1. New behaviors have been clearly identified for the particular stakeholder group and audience.
2. Critical success factors, goals and expectations have been defined and communicated.
3. A recognition and reward plan has been developed and understood by the leadership team.
4. Monetary funds have been appropriated to be used in the program.
5. Employee morale, satisfaction and motivation is monitored and evaluated.
6. The rate of successful change is tracked over time.

Performance Driver Track: Business Process

The Change Champion – Business Process

Lead and direct the development of the business processes track.

This is performed at Level 1: Strategy.

Description

One of the most significant tasks to winning the game is the change champion. The change champion is an inspiring leader who turns the vision into action. The task of the change champion is to use his or her leadership skills to guide and direct the activities in the business process track of work. This starts by thinking through the change vision in terms of the value that is provided and enhanced throughout the business process from end-to-end and within the scope of the change initiative. The change champion of the business process needs to understand the relationship between the processes that are being changed and those that are not within the scope of the change. A change in one area of the process will have some effects on the other processes. Another chief concern that the change champion will face is maintaining business continuity and current service levels throughout the project and during the transition period.

The change champion will need to understand the business requirements and capabilities when leading his or her team. The business processes are greatly influenced by the technical capabilities of software applications, systems and infrastructure. Likewise, appropriate staffing levels and competencies need to be defined to adequately function within the process to meet desired service levels and key performance indicators.

The change champion of the business process will be responsible for leading the team through the change vision in terms of how the business processes are designed to support the mission. Then, the leader will describe the vision in a way that is clearly defined and understood by the employees. It is the responsibility of the change champion to influence others to achieve the vision and accomplish the mission. The change champion motivates subordinates by providing them with a deep sense of purpose and direction to plan, design, develop and implement the changes defined by the tasks. It is the leader who sets the goals and priorities with total clarity. Likewise, it is up to the leader to define and maintain the standards and guiding principles in which the team operates.

Desired Outcomes
To enhance and align the business processes to support and sustain the vision.

Inputs
The defined pain points or the opportunities that triggered the commissioning of the change initiative.

Tools and Techniques
1. Communicate: Have honest discussions about the threats and opportunities, and give dynamic and convincing reasons to get people talking and thinking about how to change effectively.
2. Role-modeling: Get involved in shaping change through your actions.
3. Reward: Recognize and reward new behaviors and people who help meet the targets.

Metrics
Mission success rate: This metric is calculated by the percentage of tasks in the track of work that succeeded in meeting the desired outcomes divided by the number of tasks.

Planning Considerations
The change champion of the business process track does not need to have academic credentials, certifications or technical competencies around business process management. However, there are specific characteristics that each change champion should possess. These character traits are not as much about specific competencies of Six Sigma, process management, or metrics management, but rather they focus on the ability to lead

employees to carry out their assigned tasks in order to complete the project's mission within a specific time frame, and achieve the desired outcomes. Listed in Appendix B is an evaluation assessment that is used to select and assess the change champion. This assessment evaluates twenty leadership characteristics needed for this role. The specific function of the business process change champion is to address the end-to-end workflow defined in the change initiative. Simply put, the role is developed to guide the fundamental rethinking and redesign of business processes to achieve dramatic improvements in critical measures of performance, such as cost, quality, service and speed to add value to the customer and the business.

Validation of Outcomes
1. Were there frequent and honest discussions with the team members about the potential threats and an examination of the opportunities that should be taken?
2. Did the change champion describe the change vision in terms that could be easily understood and acted upon?
3. Was there an emotional commitment among the project team track that built a strong team coalition with support and guidance from the change champion?
4. Were obstacles identified and removed, allowing the project team to perform their task efficiently and effectively?
5. Were there defined goals and measures in place and clearly understood by project team members performing each key task?

Value Chain

Identify and define the value chain.

This is performed at Level 1: Strategy.

Description

One of the first activities is to identify and understand the value chain within the business. A value chain is described as all of the activities that are performed within the business process that provides value or importance to the organization and their customers. It often differentiates your organization among the other competitors. To start, the leadership will need to understand why the organization and the customer place value on a particular activity. Once there is common agreement of the value, the next question is how value is created. Is value created by a unique, differentiating factor performed within the organization, or is it cost, speed or other variables? Finally, the leadership will then need to understand what needs to be done to create or sustain the value. Without a firm understanding of the value creation elements, the project may unknowingly reduce or eliminate the value by altering the essential elements that created it in the first place. Documenting or mapping the value chain can greatly benefit the change initiative by indicating those activities that will be targeted for change and those that will not be addressed during the project. A value-chain analysis looks at every step a business goes through, from input of raw materials to delivery to the end user. The goal is to deliver maximum value for the least possible total cost.

Desired Outcomes

The goal of these activities is to offer the customer a level of value that exceeds the cost of the activities, thereby resulting in a profit margin.

Inputs
Leadership will have a common understanding of the vision for change and the overall value that this change will bring to the organization and their clients.

Tools and Techniques
- Map the value chain and vertical linkages
- Service/product-oriented analysis – determines business and customer value drivers
- Organizational culture assessment – determines current behaviors
- Map current state key business processes
- Identify the competencies of the employees supporting the processes

Metrics
Use the balanced scorecard to measure value. The balanced scorecard examines four key perspectives: learning and growth, business process, customer perspective and financial perspective.

Planning Considerations
When performing a value-chain analysis, it is important to understand the other activities that support the value chain:
- The organizational infrastructure: organizational culture, structure and control systems.
- Human capital: job roles, reporting relationships, competency development, and selection and fit.
- Technology deployment: technologies that support value-creating activities
- Knowledge management: business intelligence, analytics and decision-making

A value-chain diagram is useful to analyze the organization's core competencies and the activities in which it can pursue a competitive advantage as follows:

- Cost advantage: by better understanding costs and squeezing them out of the value-adding activities. These may include economies of scale, linkages among activities, interrelationships among business units, and regulatory compliance factors.

- Differentiation: by focusing on those activities associated with core competencies and capabilities in order to perform them better than competitors. These may include vision, core values, organizational culture, knowledge creation and sharing, and integration and synergy.

Value is a perception that can be viewed in many different ways. There is the perception of value derived from the technical capabilities that can be performed, thereby saving time by allowing systems to perform tasks that were performed by people. There is the economic perception where change could reduce cost by making products and services less expensive. Then there is the psychological perspective that provides value by providing personalized customer service. The challenge is to find the sweet spot where all of these perspectives meet and can be satisfied. This aids in getting buy-in and support from all of the key stakeholders.

Validation of Outcomes
1. Information and knowledge is used to improve competitiveness and differentiates the organization's products and services.
2. Operational costs have been reduced.
3. Operational efficiency and effectiveness have improved such as quality of service/products, innovation and adaptability to change.
4. A segment value analysis identified areas for improvement.

Business Policies and Rules

Identify internal controls that may influence the change.

This is performed at Level 1: Strategy.

Description

Business policies are guidelines statements that define the scope and area of influence and control that determine which decisions can be taken by subordinates within the organization. It permits the lower-level management to deal with the problems and issues without consulting top-level management every time a decision is required. Some business policies are developed in response to a particular situation that may have had the potential to place the organization at-risk. Other business policies are developed and implemented to standardize and control operational procedures to ensure consistency. However, policies that may have minimized risk or established working standards may no longer be applicable. Over time, the factors that once influenced the situation may have changed, no longer creating a risk. The policy subsequently may become a limiting factor or even a barrier to sustaining operational performance.

A business rule is an operation statement that defines or constrains aspects of the business operation and almost always resolves to either a true or false decision. Business rules are used to influence and control the behaviors of the business. These rules can apply to people, processes or technology systems within the organization and are put into place to help the organization achieve its goals. An example of a business rule may state that contracts over two million dollars will require legal review, or payment terms must be net thirty days. Business rules are often informal, or even unwritten. The informality of these rules can create a great deal of confusion to misinterpreting the intent. Over time, these rules may evolve into a completely different meaning and be treated as policy. To avail such confusion, rules should be well-documented to ensure the purpose and intent is understood.

Desired Outcomes
All of the business policies and business rules within the scope of the change initiative have been identified and evaluated to support the change goals.

Inputs
A thorough understanding of the change vision, goals and the value chain.

Tools and Techniques
- Document analysis
- Focus group
- Analysis compliance
- Interview
- Observation
- Requirements workshop
- Reverse engineering
- Surveys and assessments

Metrics
Policy and rule influence: Identify each business policy and business rule that relates to the change initiative. Determine if each policy or rule influences control, quality, cost or flexibility. Then, determine the impact that each policy and rule has on supporting the change vision.

Planning Considerations
Identify the business policies and documented rules that are within the scope of the change initiative. An effective business policy or business rule must have the following features:
1. Specific: The policy or rule should be specific. If it is uncertain, then the implementation will become difficult.
2. Clear: The policy or rule must be unambiguous. It should avoid use of jargons and connotations. There should be no misunderstandings in following the policy.

3. Reliable and consistent: The Policy must be uniform enough so that it can be efficiently followed by the subordinates.
4. Appropriate: The policy or rule should be appropriate to the present organizational goal.
5. Simple: The policy or rule should be simple and easily understood by all in the organization.
6. Inclusive and comprehensive: In order to have a wide scope, a policy or rule must be comprehensive.
7. Flexible: The policy or rule should be flexible in operation/ application. This does not imply that a policy or rule should always be altered, but it should be wide in scope so as to ensure that the line managers use them in repetitive/routine scenarios.
8. Stable: The policy or rule should be unwavering; else it will lead to indecisiveness and uncertainty in minds of those who look to it for guidance.

Use a variety of techniques to gather and analyze the policies and rules that will influence the initiative.

Validation of Outcomes
1. Operational policies around people and organization, business process, technical, and information and intellectual capital that are within the scope of the change initiative have been identified and reviewed by the leadership team.
2. Business rules that influence the change initiative have been gathered. Unwritten rules need to be documented to ensure the intent of the rule.
3. Operational policies and business rules that adversely alter the control, quality, cost or flexibility of the business in achieving the desired goal will be reviewed and adjusted accordingly.

Compliance

Identify regulatory and industry compliance areas.

This is performed at Level 1: Strategy.

Description

The term compliance is applied in many disciplines, and is often used to denote and demonstrate adherence of a set of defined rules that will change the way the business operates. Regulatory compliance is pervasive in nearly all aspects of business these days no matter the industry. Governance, risk and compliance concerns have become business-critical imperatives. Senior managers are focusing on these compliance concerns because of their impact on all aspects of business operations. Efforts to comply with regulatory requirements must be supported by IT systems, business processes, the organizational reporting relationship and even the organizational culture. During the change initiative, the project team must not only determine existing compliance rules in their design, but also anticipate future compliance issues that may be on the horizon.

Senior leaders must take a proactive stance to identify and comply with these regulations; leaders must consider the impact of change before it actually hits them. That kind of foresight positions the project team to adapt by changing systems and processes to get ahead of reform, and their competition. Uncertainty, issue convergence and other factors beyond the organization's control will continue to transform the industry and business operations in the foreseeable future. That is acceptable if the organization is prepared to respond to change quickly and efficiently. Understand that regulatory compliance can be transformational. Knowing how it impacts your organization and knowing what to do about it enables leaders to use those changes to their advantage.

Desired Outcomes

Validate that the change initiative addresses and complies with the various governmental and industry regulations.

Inputs

Identify the value chain and the scope of the change initiative.

Tools and Techniques

- Develop a regulatory and compliance checklist
- Establish a regulatory and compliance audit process
- Review current regulatory and compliance-related policies and procedures
- Interview key employees within the organization
- Conduct a gap analysis and develop a gap closure plan

Metrics

Select measures that relate to the specific area of compliance and measure it against a key performance indicator. There are several ways to measure compliance:

- Baseline comparisons are used to measure actual performance after and before the implementation.
- Benchmarks are used to compare other areas that have similar characteristics.
- Randomized controlled trials use a pre-selected control group that has identical characteristics to the target group.
- Comparison group studies use groups with similar characteristics and examine the difference between the groups.
- Standards are pre-defined, minimum acceptable levels of performance, including service and quality standards.
- Targets are quantifiable performance levels set for a date in the future.
- Trends provide comparisons with earlier time periods and can show whether or not a sustained impact over time has been achieved.

Planning Considerations

Listed below are some of the general practices that should be followed when dealing with regulatory compliance during a change initiative. Each type of regulation or compliance will have its own specific requirements that will need to be addressed:

- Change Management: Change management is a critical part of regulatory compliance because of the changes in business processes, roles, reporting relationships, software applications, security access and data. There needs to be a high degree of control and access of information built into the process and applications, especially when dealing with financial and healthcare related regulations. An emphasis on changing culture is critical to complying with the regulations.
- Confidentiality: It is recommended that confidential information should not be exposed to unauthorized entities. The technical architectural principles with respect to cloud computing and mobility access may increase the risk of unauthorized access. The use of acceptable encryption technologies and algorithms to ensure that data is only divulged to authorize individuals should be supported.
- Availability: Outlined in the organization's disaster recovery and business continuity plan is the availability of critical financial and other data to authorized individuals. This should include resistance to cyber attack, the use of reliable data storage devices, off-site storage, and failover mechanisms such as clustering.
- Access Controls: Most IT administrators support the use of role-based access. However, conflicts may occur when the organization supports cross-functional and high-performing teams not defined by the role. An organizational culture that supports adaptive and constructive behaviors encourages collaboration and sharing of information to make more informed decisions. The rules on accessibility may not always be defined within the application, but rather by policy to the extent defined by regulation.
- Auditing and Logging: One critical feature of IT controls is the auditing and logging of events in systems that process sensitive data. It is important to make sure that relevant system events are

logged, such as shutdowns, restarts, or unusual events. This means that access lots need to be secure, and the logs should not reveal any of the information the system is trying to protect, thus potentially exposing it to unauthorized individuals.

The creation of a separate audit group can add value to the project by auditing the compliance to the organizational governance processes. This works best if the organization has a robust framework and program in place. Then, it has the foundation to ensure internal controls are in place to comply with laws and regulations with changes in reporting relationships, job/position responsibilities, changes within the newly defined business processes, and changes with technical systems and applications. This separate auditing group can develop a framework that not only promotes more efficient, collaborative compliance-related processes, but it also ultimately minimizes the instances of noncompliance, enables early identification of systemic issues, and gives the project leadership team and the organizational leadership a view of the state of corporate compliance.

Validation of Outcomes
1. Regulatory and compliance issues are proactively addressed and factored into the initiative.
2. Focus is on changing the behaviors and driving the organizational culture to reinforce the compliance.
3. Regulatory and compliance checklists and audits are in place.
4. A compliance and ethics officer is assigned.
5. The creation of a separate audit group to support the change team.

High-Level Business Requirements

Identify the necessities needed to support the business.

This is performed at Level 2: Tactical.

Description

Business requirements are the critical activities of an enterprise that must be performed to meet the organizational objective(s) while remaining solution independent. Business requirements are defined by the business user as conditions to accomplish specific tasks to meet explicit needs and goals for both the business and the customer. Business requirements are generally defined at a high or broad level. These business requirements may also be defined within system requirements such as business processes, human resources planning and technical functional requirements. These requirements are based upon the organization's current capabilities to function at a specific performance level. Constraints are imposed by the current environment, such as staffing levels, competency levels of the employees, technologies, organizational culture, physical environment and other factors that establish the overall capabilities of performance.

Many project managers have a process and tools in place to gather business requirements. There are many different names for the tools used for this process: business needs specification, requirements specification or, simply, business requirements. A Business Requirements Document details the business needs to enable a solution for a project, including the documentation of customer needs and expectations.

The most common objectives of the Business Requirements Document are:

- To provide a foundation to communicate business requirements to be translated into technical specifications for coding and configuration.

- To describe how the customer and business needs will be met by the proposed solution.
- To establish or maintain a level of quality or service level
- To gain agreement with stakeholders.
- To meet specific compliance standards
- To provide input into the next phase for the project.

The Business Requirements Document is important because it is the foundation for all subsequent project deliverables, describing what inputs and outputs are associated with each process and system function. The document defines the conditions that are critical to service-level agreements (SLAs) and key performance indicators (KPIs), which describe the voice of the customer. The Business Requirements Document describes what the functionality would look like from a business perspective.

Desired Outcomes
A documented understanding of the current and desired customer, and business requirements in which to drive change.

Inputs
An understanding of the value chain and governance (policies, rules and compliance) that will define the business requirements.

Tools and Techniques
- Interviewing
- Documenting use cases
- Analyzing documents and reports
- Business-process modeling

Metrics
Business requirements factor: The number of requirements per person over a given period of time.

Planning Considerations

The Business Requirements Document should distinguish itself between the business solutions and the technical solution. When examining the business solution, the Business Requirement Document should answer the question, "What does the business want to do?" For example, the business wants to increase mobility access to the sales force in the field by providing near real-time sales and order information. The technical solution should be able to support the business solution by providing cloud computing and iPad devices with wireless capability. More detailed business requirements will be needed as more information is gathered from the tactical activities and tasks. It is a common mistake to transition from high-level business requirements to detailed business requirements. Although it may appear to be a natural step, there are many questions that still need to be answered at the tactical level, such as: What are the goals of providing mobility, what will be the acceptable performance levels required and what are the compliance requirements that need to be satisfied for remote access of data? Until those tactical questions are answered, the project team would be incapable of determining the detailed business rules.

Validation of Outcomes

1. Requirements are described in business terms that key stakeholders can understand.
2. Current and future-state business requirements are gathered and documented where gaps can be identified.
3. The performance metrics have been defined that influence the business requirements.
4. Capabilities and constraints have been identified that influence the business requirements.
5. The information needed to support the business requirements has been determined.

Identify and Document Key Business Processes

Ensure standards are maintained.

This is performed at Level 2: Tactical.

Description

Some work activities are more critical than other areas to sustain the business; these are considered key or critical processes. Sending out invoices to customers, paying employees and gathering customer requirements are examples of some of the many critical activities that have to be performed the same way each and every time. Getting those wrong will cause a delay in getting paid, employees to become upset and stressed, and customers to become unsatisfied. Other activities like scheduling employee training, running reports or performing administrative tasks, although important for the smooth operation of the business, are not considered critical to the business operation. Like a surgeon conducting an operation, the key procedure has to be performed the same each and every time. Although business processes are not life or death decisions, it may mean the long-term sustainability of the organization. In order to maintain consistency, these key or critical processes need to be identified and documented so that employees, new and old, will perform the task the same way.

Documenting key or critical processes takes the form of written narratives and procedures, as well as task and workflow diagrams. The narrative description should illustrate all of the details of the activity: when it is triggered, the quality of the output, the work steps, the types of decisions and other pertinent details. Identifying and documenting key processes are valuable for disaster recovery and business continuity after a major disaster. Some federal, state or industry regulations dictate which processes need to be identified and documented. The Sarbanes-Oxley act (SOX 404) requires documentation to ensure compliance. The International Standards Organization (ISO) requires documentation for certification of quality standards. Likewise, many of the other quality award criteria require documenting business processes. Documented processes should not be used to control or limit the ability of the staff to effectively meet the needs of the customer, unless of course it is controlled by regulation or law. Remember that business processes are guidelines to standardize how work is performed and flows through the organization, not strict rules.

Desired Outcomes
Key/critical business processes, those essential to the operation of the business, have been identified and documented to a level of detail.

Inputs
The value chain, business rules, regulatory compliance, and business policies.

Tools and Techniques
- Interviews and group discussions
- Process workshops
- Policy and regulatory reviews

Metrics
Key/critical process metric: The identification and documentation of a process that is essential to the business in terms of mission critical (providing value to the product or service), health and safety, or regulatory compliance or mandate. Key processes may also be identified through a Pareto analysis (i.e., using the 80/20 rule) based on volume, cycle time or number of persons required to perform the process.

Planning Considerations
Gaining a common understanding of the end-to-end process is often the most challenging part of documenting the process. Often, there are several work exceptions that arise over time, called a workaround. Short cuts taken to speed up last minute requests, substitute parts, alternate approvers, and make changes to the product are some of the many exceptions that may cause an employee to deviate from the standard.

When these exceptions become frequent, they can be confused with the norm. Soon, employees believe that this process is the standard. Changes in technologies, such as new automated software, may create changes in the process. Caution should be taken to ensure the new technology will not be designed to support a flawed process.

When these changes are not coordinated, then the documented process may become out-of-date. To avoid confusion, it is recommended to conduct a process review workshop where key stakeholders can discuss each activity and step. Key or critical processes need to be documented from their starting point to their end point. Remember that the outcome of the process should provide value to the customer. These diagrams should show major activities, tasks and work steps, including decision points. Narrative descriptions are used to describe the process and the requirements needed to support the organization and to guide the employee in their job.

Validation of Outcomes
1. The key/critical process is proven to be essential to the business in terms of:
   a. Providing value to the customer in product or service
   b. Essential to the health and safety of the employees and customers
   c. A federal, state or industry regulatory compliance or mandate
2. The key/critical process has been agreed to and approved by the senior leadership to be accurate and complete.
3. The process has been identified and documented to include a narrative description and detailed diagrams.
4. The processes are defined to the task level using swim lanes to indicate activities by function or role.
5. The process documentation is stored in a central repository where it is accessible to all employees.

Analyze Business Processes

Identify value to the customers by reducing non-value added activities.

This is performed at Level 2: Tactical.

Description

Work should flow seamlessly through the organization from end to end as the work transforms from a raw material to the finished product. To analyze the business process means to assess the performance and quality of the work as it transitions throughout the business. Key performance indicators or KPIs define the level of quality that should be achieved based upon the customer or end user's requirements. Service-level agreements or SLAs define the performance level or time that is required for specific activities and tasks to be completed along the process.

There are many areas that can be measured throughout the process, but not everything needs to be measured. Only the tasks that impact value to the customer of that activity are considered key performance indicators. The organization may choose to change their KPIs as they focus on specific aspects of the process or when quality standards change. There are generally a few KPIs that are tracked at one time to avoid confusion.

Service-level agreements are expectations set by the organization as components are brought together to make the final product, or when customers require a timely delivery. Automating certain aspects of the process will shorten service levels.

These SLAs do not have to be formal documents, but rather verbal commitments to deliver products or services within a defined time period, such as the promise to deliver a pizza in thirty minutes or less, or their money back. Service levels can change by the number of employees supporting the task, the number of decision points within the process, or other waiting points. SLAs are generally measured in time.

The process should minimize the use of any non-value added tasks to improve efficiency. Value should be determined by the customer and any regulatory compliance requirement.

Desired Outcomes

The key performance indicators and service-level agreements have been identified for all Level 3 business processes. (Task level with swim lanes)

Inputs

Customer requirements define the performance and quality standards. Regulatory compliance and business rules aid in analyzing the business process.

Tools and Techniques

- Map the critical processes to Level 3
- Conduct a SWOT analysis
- Review regulatory compliance impact to the process
- Review business rules for impact to the process
- Review SLA's and KPI's

Metrics

SLA metrics include cost/effort ratio – the expense that is associated to produce a task in a given time expressed as effort. Other metrics may consider workload to determine utilization, or time span to measure time to market. KPI metrics include quality/cost – the level of defined quality based upon the cost to achieve and maintain the level of quality.

Planning Considerations

Determine which business processes to analyze. Identify the requirements for the business process such as the inputs, outputs and triggering events. Use group sessions to validate and refine the information. Look for signs of process inefficiency or imbalance, such as long queues, long wait times or large work backlogs. Also, look for underutilized functions and work cells. Areas that go for long periods without work are also indicative of a process that is out of balance.

Document the business process by placing activities and tasks into swim lanes. Decompose the high level tasks by breaking them down into their constituent subtasks and operations. This will show an overall structure of the main user tasks. At a lower level it is desirable to show the workflows, decision points, volumes, process times, and wait time to determine overall efficiency.

In addition, determine if all of the activities are focused on meeting the overall objective of the process. Compare the results from individual interviews and surveys. Look for inconsistencies. For instance, does one step in the process deliver something to the next step that is not used in that step?

Identify activities and task outputs that are unnecessary and do not provide value to the customer. Create a future-state process and compare this process flow with the existing process. Identify gaps between the current and future state. Develop a gap closure plan that will provide efficiency while sustaining current capabilities across adjoining processes.

Validation of Outcomes
1. Business processes are documented in maps and narrative descriptions.
2. Key performance indicators (KPIs) are identified and defined based upon customer and business requirements.
3. Service-level agreements (SLAs) are indentified and defined based upon customer and business requirements.
4. Non-value adding tasks have been reduced or eliminated.
5. Measures are used to continually monitor the performance of the process.

Identify Business Rules

Rules are the process gatekeepers that need to be incorporated in the process.

This is performed at Level 3: Operational.

Description

A business rule is a statement that defines or constrains some aspect of the business. It is intended to assert business structure, or to control or influence the behavior of the business. They transcend single processes and are based upon business requirements. The business rules can apply to people, process, technology and the handling of information and knowledge; they reinforce the beliefs and goals of the leaders.

The rules pertain to any of the constraints that apply to the behavior of people in the organization, from guidelines for working overtime hours to restrictions on using social networking. From the information system perspective, it pertains to what information is captured and shared, to the value that is placed on those facts. That is, the significance the organization places on the quality of information to guide the business.

Business rules are less formal than policies and are often implied rather than written. Tacit knowledge supports business rules. There can be an understanding among employees of what acceptable behavior is, or what is needed to get the job done within the guidelines that are the business rules.

Desired Outcomes

Have business rules identified, documented and easily changed by the user. Business rules can be embedded into the procedures that support the process and may be configured into supporting technologies.

Inputs

Core values, vision, goals, defined metrics and documented processes.

Tools and Techniques
- Review business and client requirements
- Conduct a business rules analysis

Metrics
Use the key performance indicators and service-level agreements to determine which business rules are needed to be effective.

Planning Considerations
Business rules are often used by leaders as directives to provide guidance or direction to the employees. Leaders may convey these directives via a memo, an e-mail or through conversations in meetings. Business leaders may create a business rule to provide a solution for a temporary problem. An issue occurs when the problem is resolved but the rule is not removed. These outdated business rules may decrease both performance and service-level agreements.

Business rules need to be flexible, adapting to the changes within the business. When treated like expectations, employees understand what should be expected and what actions exceed acceptable behavior while conducting business. These rules should be openly discussed and shared among employees to establish guidelines to achieve the quality of business that is expected.

Validation of Outcomes
1. Business rules are aligned to the key performance indicators and the service-level agreements.
2. Business rules are documented where possible.
3. Business rules that are outdated are purged and communicated that a change has taken place.

Detailed Business Requirements

Identify those conditions that support the specific details within the process.

This is performed at Level 3: Operational.

Description

Detailed business requirements focus on the day-to-day business operation. Every activity and task in the business operation is created in response to a business need and the needs of the customer. These needs change as the business and their customers mature, or as external conditions change, such as new technical capabilities from mobile devices, a change in the economic environment, or a shift in social networking that creates a greater visibility into the company and the products or services.

To understand these influencing factors, a detailed business requirements analysis should be conducted. This is the process of discovering, analyzing, defining and documenting the requirements that are related to a specific business objective. A good business requirements analysis helps stakeholders to better understand the business needs and break them into detailed, specific requirements that everyone agrees on.

There are four main categories of requirements: functional, operational, technical and transitional.

- **Functional Requirements** – These define how a product/ service/solution should function from the end user's perspective. They describe the features and functions with which the end user will interact directly.
- **Operational Requirements** – These define operations that must be carried out in the background to keep the product or process functioning over a period of time.

- **Technical Requirements** – These define the technical issues that must be considered to successfully enhance the business process, improve customer visibility, or enhance the product or service.
- **Transitional Requirements** – These are the steps needed to implement the new product or process smoothly.

Desired Outcomes

To identify, define and document the detailed business requirements. The key stakeholders should gain a consensus of each detailed business requirement identified.

Inputs

Understand the high-level business requirements, business rules and the performance goals.

Tools and Techniques

- Interviews
- Focus groups
- Use cases
- Conference room pilots
- Building prototypes

Metrics

Acceptance ratio: The number of detailed business requirements to meet or exceed customer or end user needs.

Planning Considerations

Start by identifying the key stakeholders, customers and possibly the end users of the product or service. These people may be internal or external to the organization. It is essential that you know who will be satisfied by the requirement. There may be a compromise as to which requirements need to be satisfied for a particular group. Other considerations may include the impact on existing systems or processes beyond the scope of the initiative. Still, other considerations may include cost, time and quality variables.

Capture the key stakeholder's requirements. There are several methods that can be used depending upon the size and scope of the target population. Surveys, interviews, focus groups, pilots and prototypes are some of the many ways that information can be collected.

Divide the detailed requirements into groups to make it easier to manage. These groups are typically operational processes, functional work steps, technical capabilities and transitional activities.

Once the detailed requirements have been grouped, the project team needs to translate the business requirements into functional specifications; prioritize the requirements from the must have to the nice to have needs, and analyze the detailed requirements to determine if it is feasible based upon the current or proposed capability that will fit with the key performance indicators and service-level agreements. Any issues should be resolved by the business and project leaders. After each detailed requirement has been analyzed, it then should be well-documented. Upon completion of this process, the document should be signed off by the business and project leaders.

Validation of Outcomes
1. Key stakeholders, customers and end users have been identified.
2. Detailed business requirements have been sorted and analyzed.
3. An understanding of the capabilities and limitations of the business to meet the detailed business requirements have been determined.
4. The detailed business requirements have been documented and signed off by the key business leaders.

Identify the Activities and Tasks

Define the actions that need to be performed by the job role/ position.

This is performed at Level 3: Operational.

Description

Processes are partitioned into activities and tasks at the operational level. They are aligned in sequential order from the triggering event that starts the process, to the end point where an output is defined. Also included are decision points that determine which set of activities or tasks need to be performed based upon a given situation. Processes are illustrated in what are called process maps. These maps divide the activities and tasks into rows called swim lanes, much like a swimming pool. A detailed process map aids employees in determining who will perform what activities or tasks; the order in which they are performed; the type of decisions that need to be made; and who to pass the work product to when completed.

An activity is a major unit of work to be completed in achieving the objectives of a process. An activity is made up of a series of related tasks to complete an action, and tasks are made up of work steps. It has precise starting and ending points, incorporates a set of tasks to be completed, consumes resources and results in work products. An activity may have a precedence relationship with other activities. For example, finish-to-start, start-to-start and finish-to-finish.

A task is the smallest unit of work subject to management accountability. A task is a well-defined work assignment usually assigned to one person. Related tasks are grouped to form activities. In order to perform the task to a consistent standard, a procedure of defined work steps is documented.

Desired Outcomes
Activities and tasks are identified, mapped within a process and analyzed to improve performance and provide value.

Inputs
Clearly defined inputs and outputs for the process; defined key performance indicators and service-level agreements; and business requirements.

Tools and Techniques
- Collaborative workshops
- SWOT analysis
- Map activities and tasks into swim lanes

Metrics
Identify the key performance indicators (KPI) and service-level agreement (SLA) for each process.

Planning Considerations
Undocumented processes seem to take on a life of their own; everyone appears to have a different understanding of what the process is intended to do. The employees who work within a process can describe "what" they do with precise clarity; however, it may become a little more difficult when asking them "how" the process works. Then asks the same employees "why" the process is needed to function that way, and you will get blank stares and puzzled looks. The employees have a strong comprehension of their tasks or work steps, but often do not have knowledge of the downstream impact of their actions. Those who have been associated with the organization for awhile hear anecdotal stories and certain assumptions of how things are "supposed to work," but many times they are false. Acts of well-meaning intentions may create extra work for those who receive the product or service downstream of the process. It is not until the process is well-documented and shared within a collaborative work session that the true understanding of the requirements will become clear.

The most effective way to document a process is to gather everyone in the same room who is involved with performing the tasks and work steps. These are not just the key stakeholders, rather everyone including the administrative assistant. Although these may be lower-level workers, they often perform a vital part in making the process work. It may be the administrative assistant who runs a report, directs a customer's call, or approves a workflow request from the boss.

Start by defining the starting point of the process. This is what triggers the process, such as a customer request or a regularly scheduled event, like the end of a pay period. Then define the end point of the process, the hand off, or the finished product. Define the outcome of the process in terms your customer would understand. Describe the level of performance and quality desired. Next, ask the group what the first activity or task is, followed by the next and so on. Document each activity or task using a Post-it note on a large piece of paper on the wall. Create a "swim lane" for each group or role where the work flows. This may include groups such as sales, procurement, financial, administration and even the customer. You will find that as the team identifies the tasks, there are others who may come before. The Post-it note will allow you to move the task to the proper sequence.

Identify decision points that may exist between activities or tasks. There may be multiple paths made by a decision defined by a rule. There are three types of decision rules: And, Or and XOR. The table defines the various rules.

And	Splits the process flow into two or more parallel paths.
Or	Follows one or more possible paths as a result of the decision made.
XOR	Follows one, but not more than one of the possible paths.

The next task is to identify the technical systems and other tools that enhance the process. Indicate which activity or task will access a specific technology. These systems may be large, enterprise systems, an internet application accessed on a mobile phone or an excel spreadsheet.

Documenting these systems will aid in determining the existing capabilities and aid in defining the technical system requirements to enhance the process. The bottom swim lane is used to indicate the technical systems that support the activities or tasks.

A well-documented and mapped process will assist the project team to determine potential problems, such as steps that are disconnected, an overly complex process, or identification of non-value added activities.

A process analysis is a technique that is used to determine the overall value added activities and identify those tasks that do not produce value. Ideally, each task should enhance or add value in terms that the customer would appreciate. Multiple approval steps and filing paperwork do not add value for the customer. These tasks may be required for the organization, but are viewed as non-value added. Seek ways to reduce the wait time, push decisions down to the lowest level of authority, and empower employees to make decisions on quality.

Validation of Outcomes
1. Document business processes on maps that illustrate the workflow through the organization.
2. Identify which group or role performs specific activities or tasks.
3. Identify key decisions and map the path for each decision.
4. Have a documented narrative that describes the process, the conditions in which it works, and the level of quality and performance required.
5. Ensure that the employees who work in the process understand the process end to end, along with the implications of their actions.
6. Analyze the process to reduce or eliminate the non-value added activities.

Work Steps

Define the steps to perform the activity consistently.

This is performed at Level 4: Functional.

Description

Work steps are the most detailed level of process documentation. Tasks are made up of several work steps used to guide the user through each step of the process. I will use the task of brewing a pot of coffee as an example. Here are the work steps: 1) fill the pot with cold water to the designated mark, 2) place a paper filter into the metal basket inside of the coffee pot, 3) measure six tablespoons of coffee and place it into the paper filter, 4) place the top cover onto the metal basket and the lid on the coffee pot, 5) plug the coffee maker into the electrical outlet, and 6) once the coffee has stopped percolating, pour the coffee into a cup. These six steps provide the details that guide the user to consistently brew coffee. Although these steps provide consistency, it does not address deviations in the requirements, for instance more or less cups of coffee, a stronger or weaker brew of coffee, different flavors, a hotter cup, or iced coffee. Likewise, the work steps do not address service-level agreements, as in how many cups of coffee can be brewed over a given period of time. They also do not address the key performance indicators, for instance, if the quality of the coffee consistently meets the customer's requirements. Therefore, in addition to the documented work steps, the worker will need to continually understand and respond to the unique and changing customer requirements and have internal controls in place for temperature, freshness and quantity consistently produced.

Desired Outcomes

Documented work-steps procedures.

Inputs

Understanding of customer requirements; documented processes, activities, and tasks; goals and objectives; key performance indicators, and service-level agreements.

Tools and Techniques

- Use documented process maps and process narratives to provide scope and structure.
- Collaborative work sessions to identify and validate the work steps.

Metrics

Ease and simplicity: The work steps should be easy to read and understandable for the average person to complete the task with a level of proficiency.

Planning Considerations

Not all work steps need to be documented. We perform many different tasks each day which are second nature to us, like brewing coffee, opening a Word document on our laptop, or searching the Internet. These tasks and their associated work steps are not critical to the business in terms of adding value to the customers. Standardization is the determining factor in documenting work steps. In business, we want to deliver quality products and services consistently to our customers. Regulatory compliance or safety standards may also require the work steps to be documented.

Each of the work steps should include key decision points. There are many decisions that we make for each task we perform. A key decision is one that involves commitment of resources, such as money, time, people or equipment. A key decision may also include risk mitigation, a decision that may cause the customer or the organization to diminish quality, increase cost, involve more people, or jeopardize the relationship.

Documenting work steps should not be a substitute for training. The work steps can act as a guide to ensure the task is performed consistently —

primarily addresses the routine or the ordinary way the task should be performed. The employee performing these tasks should <u>not</u> be a robot and follow programmed instructions. Situations change constantly and will require the employee to use skill and experience to make the most appropriate decision. Most work steps are not so rigid as to be followed to the letter of the law. The only exception is specific tasks associated to a high-reliability organization. A high-reliability organization (HRO) is an organization that has succeeded in avoiding catastrophes in an environment where normal accidents can be expected due to risk factors and complexity, such as a high loss of life or property. These organizations include the Federal Aviation Administration (FAA) during flight operations at an airport control tower; the Nuclear Regulatory Commission in designing and operating nuclear power plants; and the flight deck of an aircraft carrier. Here, these tasks and work steps must be followed exactly as described, without deviation. Fortunately, most of our tasks do not involve life or death situations; they still need to be consistent with the values and goals of the organization to prevent the loss of business.

Validation of Outcomes

1. Key tasks are identified where work steps need to be documented.
2. Decision points have been identified in the normal course of performing the task.
3. Work steps for each task provide the functional detail to the operational process and should be the logical steps to complete the task.
4. Work step descriptions are written in plain language and easy to read.

Documented Procedures

Establish the correct method of performing the activity.

This is performed at Level 4: Functional.

Description

Procedures are more than basic step-by-step instructions that provide information on how to complete ongoing tasks on a regular basis. Documentation empowers the people responsible for a process with the direction and consistency required for success far beyond the individual work steps. Well-written work steps, policies, guidelines and procedures allow employees to understand their roles, responsibilities and limits. Risks associated with activities that are of critical importance to the organization, such as quality levels, service levels, regulatory compliance requirements, legal liabilities and financial matters are mitigated by well-developed policies, guidelines and procedures.

Documented procedures assist in ensuring that repetitive processes are completed in a consistent and predictable manner. Comprehensive documentation will assist your organization in the following areas:

- Operational Needs — Written procedures ensure that operational and functional processes are performed in a consistent way that meets the organization's needs.
- Risk Management — Established procedures are an effective control activity needed to manage risk.
- Training Tool — Documented procedures assist in training existing and new personnel in performing their responsibilities.
- Promote Best Practices — Written procedures document the best way of performing tasks by determining the desirable results in methods and techniques internal and external to the organization, and documenting the lessons learned. Knowledge sharing can preserve and disseminate the organization's

experiences by passing along business and technical know-how through documentation.

Desired Outcomes
Work steps, policies, guidelines and procedures are documented in one place accessible to employees.

Inputs
Regulatory compliance guidelines, policies, business rules, business requirements and process documentation.

Tools and Techniques
- Benchmarking
- Best practice analysis
- Risk identification, analysis and avoidance
- Linking policies to procedures

Metrics
Procedure alignment: Documented procedures are current and aligned with business best practices.

Planning Considerations
Work steps answer the question of "what" is needed to complete the task. Documented procedures answer the question of "how" and in part the "why" it is performed. The procedure document, therefore, is more informative, providing employees greater knowledge when performing their jobs. Nearly anyone can be provided with well-documented work steps to perform the task within an acceptable level of performance, but not have the slightest idea why they were performing the work steps, or how the work steps achieve the desired results.

A business process is only as good as the operating procedure supporting it. The organization can have every single process, activity and task modeled and documented, but if they are not supported by sound procedures, the process will eventually fail. With proper knowledge transfer and documentation of the business procedures, leaders can ensure consistency of quality and efficiency standards. These procedures aid employees in solving problems and providing guidance with out-of-the-ordinary situations.

Organizations of all kinds use documents to convey messages both internally and externally. For an organization to stay efficient, it must develop mechanisms for controlling and organizing these documents. In fact, the International Organization for Standardization or (ISO) publishes guidelines that non-governmental organizations can use to meet quality standards.

It is recommended to put documents online to have one version to control rather than maintaining multiple copies and risk employees working from outdated procedures. Placing work steps, procedures, process maps, regulatory compliance standards, and all other supporting documents into one location linked together can make it easy for employees to make the right decisions. The goal is to provide employees with a single reference source to gain knowledge of the value produced from the process within the organization.

Validation of Outcomes
1. A procedure review and approval process has been defined and implemented.
2. A centralized online document management system is used to store and retrieve procedures.
3. Work steps, policies, procedures, business rules, regulations and other documentation is contained in one location.
4. Best practices and knowledge sharing is supported.
5. Leaders support and enforce documented procedures.

Business Activity Monitoring

Observe changes in requirements from the customer and the business.

This is performed at Level 4: Functional.

Description

Business Activity Monitoring (BAM) is a key component of business performance. Performance measurement of business processes is crucial for the ongoing success of an organization. Through real-time visibility and monitoring of every crucial business process and activity, organizations are able to act on insights gained from meeting the needs of their customers. Business Activity Monitoring allows employees to monitor levels of service and achievement of goals using key performance indicators. It is important to provide employees constructive feedback on their work so they can make adjustments as needed. Likewise, it is important to differentiate between human performance and process performance. It is not always easy to discern between the two because it takes people to make the process work.

This activity will focus on monitoring the process, providing employees with information which they can use to analyze and to make a determination on which factors will change the performance. There are many ways to monitor the activities and tasks in a process from simple observation to sophisticated statistical control systems. Whatever the system used, the primary objective is to provide quick and accurate feedback to the employees who are directly involved within the process. This feedback should also include the suppliers and customers since they are part of the process. There are many ways to display the information: charts and graphs on paper, or electronic dashboards on computers. This allows key stakeholders to respond quickly to process or business inefficiencies, ensure that operations run smoothly, and guarantee that critical business services are available.

Desired Outcomes

Activities performed within the process are achieved to the standards which have been established for the process.

Inputs

Business and customer requirements, service-level agreements (SLA), key performance indicators (KPI), performance metrics and defined goals.

Tools and Techniques

- Analytic tools (reports, dashboards)
- Capability assessments

Metrics

Operational performance: The performance information is displayed in near real time and operates within the defined standards.

Planning Considerations

As an organization becomes more complex, the ability to track operational performance becomes paramount. The correlation of business processes becomes critical to empower both management and staff to reduce errors and increase production efficiency while gaining knowledge. However, managing processes amidst ever-increasing complexity can create issues. Business processes go through maturity levels, and as they mature, the business goes through a transformation. As a result, the rules that reinforce behaviors, such as performance rewards will need to be changed. Individual departments may have set their own performance and quality standards rather than aligning to the end-to-end business processes. The organization may be rewarding individual or department performance at the risk of creating barriers in the process. A learning environment must be created to capture lessons learned and crate shared knowledge to continually improve.

Maturing business processes and technology have a direct impact on the capabilities needed by the employees to perform activities and tasks at acceptable levels. As the organization develops knowledge workers, moving away from performing administrative tasks, the level of knowledge, skill, and ability defined by the activity or task will continue to evolve, requiring the employee to continually learn.

There are a variety of metrics and measures that can be used to monitor business activities, but monitoring too many can become overwhelming to manage. The leadership should focus on key issues within the process. To effectively manage the process, the focus should be limited to a critical few, generally four metrics. Once those areas have achieved a sustainable level of performance and quality, then a new set of metrics should be selected to direct the organization's efforts to meet the goals.

> "What gets measured gets done, what gets measured and fed back gets done well, what gets rewarded gets repeated."   — John E. Jones

Validation of Outcomes
1. Feedback on performance is provided in near real time.
2. Key few, critical metrics are identified to measure and provide feedback.
3. Information is displayed using charts or graphs.
4. All members of the process have access to the feedback data.
5. Individual employee performance is separate from process performance.
6. Information can be displayed on paper, dashboards, or a variety of other methods and shared among stakeholders.

Performance Driver Track: Technology

The Change Champion – Technology

Lead and direct the technology track.

This is performed at Level 1: Strategy.

Description

One of the most significant tasks to winning the game is the change champion. The change champion is an inspiring leader that turns the vision into action. The task of the change champion is to use his or her leadership skills to guide and direct the activities in the technology alignment track of work. This starts by thinking through the change vision in terms of the value that is provided and enhanced through the principles, selection and configuration of the technology to support the scope of the change initiative and ultimately the organization.

The change champion of technology needs to understand how business processes can be enhanced by technology while maintaining the current service levels and capabilities throughout the enterprise. Technical changes in one area of the business may have a negative impact in other areas of the business. Another chief concern that the change champion will face is maintaining business continuity and current service levels throughout the project and during the transition period.

The change champion will also need to recognize the business requirements and capabilities when managing his or her team. The current staffing levels and capabilities are a factor when determining the technical requirements needed to support the initiative while at the same time maintaining current service levels to support the entire organization. Likewise, selecting new technical systems will impact the staffing levels and capabilities in the future. Other strategic decisions such as outsourcing or moving to a new platform or hardware/software vendor will influence the way this functional group operates in the future.

Technology is used to support and enhance the business processes through integration, automation and collaboration. These systems can be highly complex, requiring specific competencies. Software vendors build in best practices which may control or influence the way a process functions. There can be a tendency for the technology group to drive or dictate how the process should work. However, caution should be taken as not to deviate from the core values and vision of the change initiative. Relatively minor changes can, for example, diminish a superior customer experience by delaying or eliminating an action from taking place. These deviations may be caused by limitations in the software, provided by out-of-the-box functionality. A cost-benefit analysis and risk assessment may be required to evaluate the impact.

Some technology advancements can be so uniquely different that it would influence the organization to operate in a completely different way. A technology that may greatly enhance or change the way business is conducted is also known as disruptive technologies. Although these advancements may provide the organization with a competitive advantage, the change may not be accepted by the employees in the organization or their target customers. Examples of this may include online stores, mobile access to allow employees to work remotely, or simply automating certain processes. These changes may make good business sense, but may be rejected by the prevailing organizational culture.

The change champion of the technical alignment track that includes systems, applications, networks and infrastructures will be responsible for leading the team through the change vision in terms of how the business processes are enhanced by the technology to support the mission. Then, the leader will describe the vision in a way that is clearly defined and understood by the stakeholders. It is the responsibility of the change champion to influence others to achieve the vision and accomplish the mission. The change champion motivates subordinates by providing them with a deep sense of purpose and direction to plan, design, develop and implement the changes defined by the tasks. It is the leader who sets the goals and priorities with total clarity. Likewise, it is up to the leader to define and maintain the standards and guiding principles in which the team operates.

Desired Outcomes
To align the technology to support and sustain the vision.

Inputs
The defined pain points or the opportunities that triggered the commissioning of the change initiative.

Tools and Techniques
1. Communicate: Have honest discussions about the threats and opportunities, and give dynamic and convincing reasons to get people talking and thinking about how to effectively change.
2. Role-modeling: Get involved in shaping the change through your actions.
3. Reward: Recognize and reward new behaviors and people who help meet the targets.

Metrics
Mission success rate. This metric is calculated by the percentage of tasks in the track of work that had succeeded to meet their desired outcomes divided by the number of tasks.

Planning Considerations
The change champion of the technology track needs to understand the principles, methods and operational requirements consistent with the complexities of the IT infrastructure within the organization. In addition, there are specific characteristics that each change champion should possess. These character traits are not as much about specific competencies of Six Sigma, business intelligence, enterprise applications, or metrics management, but rather they focus on the ability to lead employees to carry out their assigned tasks in order to complete the project's mission within a specific time frame, and achieve the desired outcomes. Listed in Appendix B is an evaluation assessment that is used to

select and assess the change champion. This assessment evaluates twenty leadership characteristics needed for this role. The specific function of the technology change champion is to address the end-to-end workflow defined in the change initiative to meet customer and business requirements. Simply put, the role is developed to guide the fundamental rethinking and redesign of the business operation to achieve dramatic improvements in critical measures of performance, such as cost, quality, service and speed, to add value for the customer and the business.

Validation of Outcomes

1. Were there frequent and honest discussions with the team members about the potential threats and an examination of the opportunities that should be taken?
2. Did the change champion describe the change vision in terms that could be easily understood and acted upon?
3. Was there an emotional commitment among the project team track that built a strong team coalition with support and guidance from the change champion?
4. Were obstacles identified and removed, allowing the project team to perform their task efficiently and effectively?
5. Were there defined goals and measures in place and clearly understood by project team members performing each key task?

Technical Architectural Principles

Define the general rules and guidelines for the use and deployment of all IT resources and assets within the enterprise.

This is performed at Level 1: Strategy.

Description

Technical architecture is defined as the formal, considered plan or design that guides development or construction of business systems. It is the framework of principles, guidelines, standards, models and strategies which directs the design, construction and deployment of information technology throughout the enterprise. It is made up of a picture of the current state, a vision and blueprint of the future, and a roadmap on how to get there.

Technical Architectural Principles define the underlying general rules and guidelines for the use and deployment of all technology resources and assets across the organization. They reflect a level of consensus among the various functions of the organization and form the basis for making future technical decisions. Each technical architecture principle should be clearly related back to the business objectives and key architecture drivers. These principles should be well-documented in a basic and recommended format: Name – describe the principle clearly and concisely; Statement – provides a description of the principle; Rationale – describes the business benefits and the governance of the business operation; and Implications – highlight the requirements from both the IT and business perspective. There should be a limited number of principles so as not to overwhelm the person trying to understand them. A general rule is to keep it to twenty or less.

Desired Outcomes

Documented IT principles along with a picture of the current state, vision and blueprint of the future, and a roadmap.

112

Inputs

Technology Architecture Principles are based upon the core values, mission and vision of the organization.

Tools and Techniques
- Interviews, workshops, focus groups
- Technology roadmap
- Capacity modeling
- Quality functional deployment

Metrics

Business Capability – Technical functional capability and maturity to enhance the business process.

Planning Considerations
1. The technical solutions must be scalable to adjust to the scope and capability of the business. The architecture provides a baseline to support future business volume growth requirements.
2. The technical architecture blueprint builds a strong foundation for the future. The architecture establishes the building blocks on which future business capabilities can be built. The architecture framework should provide capabilities that can accommodate existing solutions.
3. The solution should be implemented through an approach that minimizes complexity. The architecture should be no more complex than it needs to be to satisfy business' needs. Employees should have the capabilities and requisite skills to implement and maintain the solution. The technical blueprint aids in providing an answer to solving the business problem. It builds a framework for the future, and business requirements must drive the solution definition and technology.
4. The architecture should minimize custom development. The architecture leverages off-the-shelf solutions when meeting core business requirements and uses the core capabilities of the integration and data management products as much as possible. As new business requirements develop, the project team should

look for off-the-shelf solutions to meet business needs as opposed to custom development.

5. The technical architecture is based on common standards. The solution should define consistent standards for systems integration that can be applied throughout the organization. These standards should be understandable and available to all users. Standards should be defined for reusable software components, software delivery and managing information.

Validation of Outcomes

1. Technical architectural principles are aligned to the vision and values of the organization.
2. There should be a select few principles that are well-documented (twenty or less).
3. A technology architectural blueprint and roadmap is created to define the technical vision of the future.

Cloud Computing

Leverage the capabilities of cloud computing to expand mobility.

This is performed at Level 1: Strategy.

Description

Cloud computing is a term that represents the practice of using a network of remote servers hosted on the Internet to store, manage and process data, rather than a local computer. Cloud computing is the logical next step in the evolution of the Internet by proving the means through which software applications, business processes and social networking can deliver services to anyone, wherever and whenever it is needed.

Cloud computing provides a set of hardware, networks, storage, services and interfaces that combine together to deliver many aspects of computing as a service. There are five essential characteristics that have been defined: flexibility and the ability for rapid elasticity; broad network access; on-demand self-service provisioning; resource pooling; and the billing and metering of service usage in a pay-as-you-go model. These features make it efficient for organizations to manage their IT services.

There are a variety of cloud computing models that provide specific services:

- Infrastructure as a Service (IaaS). The IaaS layer offers storage and computing resources that IT organizations can use to deliver business solutions.
- Platform as a Service (PaaS). The PaaS layer offers IT developers a platform in which they can build applications. These platforms may provide tools that are offered as a service to build services, or data access and database services, or billing services.
- Software as a Service (SaaS). In the SaaS layer, the service provider hosts the software so the business does not need to install it, manage it, or buy hardware for it. Everything is provided

115

and maintained so the business can focus on just using the services. There are many examples that use these services: web-based e-mail, blogging sites, customer relationship management (CRM) as a service, and even the many smartphone applications.

There are a variety of uses that an organization can leverage to meet the evolving needs of their business and their customers. The organization needs to determine the most effective and efficient way to manage resources. Cloud computing can completely change the way organizations use technology to operate their business and interact with customers, partners and suppliers. They have found that it can eliminate many of the complex constraints from the traditional computing environment, including space, time, power and cost.

Desired Outcomes
Cloud computing has been considered in the organization's technical architectural principles to meet current and future quality and performance requirements.

Inputs
A firm understanding of the changing business requirements and the vision of future business operations.

Tools and Techniques
- Use a decision tree such as an Ishikawa (fishbone)
- Conduct surveys and interviews
- Develop metrics to determine quality and performance
- Create a business case to perform a financial analysis

Metrics
Cloud computing risk and benefit metrics should be identified and measured. Some benefits that should be considered include low operating cost, ease of use, scalability and minimum infrastructure requirements. These are compared to some of the risks such as bandwidth limitations, security, legal requirements and service availability.

Planning Considerations

There are a number of considerations that need to be analyzed prior to moving toward or away from a cloud computing solution. First, an organization should assess its business strategy and whether a cloud computing infrastructure could integrate with the technology architecture principles. With all the convenience that cloud offers, the risk of data residing beyond your company's vicinity still can present a significant security risk to cyber attacks.

An assessment of how much risk your organization is prepared to take in order to cut costs will initially be the first factor in deciding which data and applications should be outsourced to the cloud. This is what can limit organizations to use the cloud for archival purposes rather than leveraging the full power of the virtualization of the cloud.

Another consideration is regulatory compliance management. Organizations need to understand where their data will reside, as well as who will interact with it and how. They need to understand which areas of compliance the service provider controls and how to audit against the standards and regulations to which they need to adhere.

There are many more considerations that need to be addressed when developing a cloud computing strategy for the organization. Focus on the changing business and customer requirements that will soon emerge.

From time to time, all cloud services will have outages when the system goes down. So it's important to consider the cloud provider's service record, how it compares with other providers, and what penalties or credits on costs of service apply when there are outages.

The cloud computing environment must have verified, auditable controls in place to provide assurances to the user community that it will not cause them harm. The cloud environment must be robust and complete in its defensible architecture and controls. In an effort to safeguard against security attacks, a rapid and automated defense and response system must be implemented. Malware detection, audit, and identification and access controls are some examples of verifiable protection.

System integrity in a cloud environment should rely on a number of complimentary and compensating controls, from file integrity to malicious code protection and predictable failure prevention. Integrity controls vary at each level of service models, as SaaS environments focus on application integrity such as input validation, while IaaS environments focus on file system and data base integrity.

Guidelines should be developed to provide a framework to help the organization and the project team make sound, risk-based security decisions about how to securely embrace cloud computing.

Validation of Outcomes
1. The cloud computing approach is part of the technical architecture principles.
2. Cloud computing offers many alternatives for use which should be well-defined.
3. Risks and constraints are well-documented and addressed in the approach plan.
4. Metrics and measures are identified and implemented.
5. A business case is used to validate the transition to cloud computing.

Business Continuity and Disaster Recovery

Build, test and validate continuity and recovery processes, systems and resources.

This is performed at Level 1: Strategy.

Description

There are many risks that may threaten an organization by disrupting business processes. These risks include traditional emergencies like fires, floods, earthquakes and tornados, as well as risks from physical and cyber-terrorism, cyber-crime, computer and telecommunication failures, theft, employee sabotage, and labor strife. Any one of these can be very disruptive for the business.

Business Continuity Management, or BCM, is a term that is often thought of as another way to say "disaster recovery," but it means much more. Disaster recovery was once thought of as recovering data and associated software applications that may have been lost. Business Continuity Management means ensuring the continuity or uninterrupted provision of operations and services. Business Continuity Management is an ongoing process with several different, but complementary elements. Planning for business continuity is a comprehensive process that includes disaster recovery, business recovery, business resumption and contingency planning.

Disaster recovery focuses on minimization of the emergency itself by addressing the critical systems. Business recovery focuses on restoring business processes by addressing how the critical business processes function. Business resumption focuses on returning the business back to normal by restoring or replacing equipment and buildings where the work is performed. The contingency planning process focuses on making do with what is available to keep the business operational, relying on manual processes and making do with the resources. Each one of these four areas requires a specific plan.

Major change within the organization requires a change within the four business continuity plans. As with technical architecture, software, physical environments, business processes, data, staff, and other areas, the plans must be well managed, updated and tested.

Desired Outcomes
Strategic plans for changes need to be coordinated with disaster recovery, business recovery, business resumption and contingency planning. These plans need to be updated and tested.

Inputs
- An understanding of the change vision
- Technical architecture: software, infrastructure, networks
- Process maps and narratives
- Staffing levels and organizational structure

Tools and Techniques
- Planning review sessions

Metrics
Business operation sustainability: The ability to maintain business operations in the event of a crisis or major disruption with minimal downtime over a given time period.

Planning Considerations
The duration of the recovery to resume business is the determining factor. Plans should be made based upon the duration of the recovery period. The longer the disaster, the more complex the recovery process will become. Planning should be performed in eight phases.

Phase 1: Initiation of the business continuity planning project. In this phase, the project team is brought together where the existing business continuity plans are reviewed and the requirements defined.

Phase 2: Assessing business risks and the potential impact from an emergency. During this phase, an impact assessment is performed to assess the loss of facilities, equipment, systems and people. A business risk assessment is performed to examine business processes, and financial and operational costs.

Phase 3: Preparing for a possible emergency. These tasks develop strategies for backup and recovery, personnel and supplies, and documented procedures.

Phase 4: Disaster recovery phase. This section includes the planning for handling the emergency. Emergency services such as police and fire departments are involved in the planning process which includes notification and reporting during the disaster recovery phase.

Phase 5: Business recovery phase. During this phase, the business recovery team is mobilized to assess the extent of the damage and the business impact. The team monitors the process and communicates to the key stakeholders. The team focuses on bringing the business back to normal operations.

Phase 6: Testing the business recovery plan. Test plans are created to address the various scenarios. Test data is prepared, and people are identified to perform the tests. The employees will test the accuracy of vendor contact numbers.

Phase 7: Training is performed in business recovery and resumption. Training budgets are created and approved. The training materials are developed and training schedules prepared. Training is conducted and assessed.

Phase 8: Keeping the plan up-to-date. Procedures are created to maintain the plan. Responsibilities for maintenance of each part of the plan are identified.

Validation of Outcomes
A comprehensive business continuity plan developed and modified to accept the change.

Enterprise Systems

Leverage the integration and collaboration capabilities of systems to support processes.

This is performed at Level 2: Tactical

Description

Enterprise systems are large-scale application software packages that support business processes, information flows, reporting and data analytics in large, complex organizations. Types of enterprise systems include enterprise resource planning (ERP) systems, and customer relationship management (CRM) software. Although data warehousing or business intelligence systems are enterprise-wide packaged application software often sold by software vendors, they do not directly support execution of business processes and are often excluded from the term.

Some of the factors that contribute to ERP adoption trend towards globalization, mergers and acquisitions, and the need to reduce operational costs. An ERP system may determine whether it creates a competitive advantage or becomes a corporate headache. An implementation involves a significant alteration to the existing business practices, as well as an outlay of huge capital investments. The other important factors are the issues related to reengineering the business processes and integrating the other business applications to the ERP backbone.

Senior management must play a key role in managing the change an ERP brings into an organization. Organizational commitment is paramount due to possible lengthy implementation and huge costs involved. Once implemented, an ERP system is difficult and expensive to undo. Since no single ERP solution can satisfy all business needs, organizations may have to implement custom applications in addition to the ERP software. Integrating different software packages poses a serious challenge, and the integration patchwork has been expensive and difficult to maintain.

Desired Outcomes

- Enterprise applications are configured to enhance business processes by leveraging built-in best practices.
- The features and functionality of the ERP and CRM applications are aligned to support the mission and vision of the organization.
- The business processes define the requirements of the applications.
- There should not be custom coding of the enterprise applications, but leverage the features and functionality that is offered.

Inputs

A cost/benefit analysis has been performed to determine quality and performance delivered in a cost efficient approach. Future-state business processes are well-defined and documented.

Tools and Techniques

- Option engineering
- Cost/benefit analysis
- Impact analysis
- Best practice analysis

Metrics

Real-time accessibility: Information is entered and accessible in near real time to make current and informed decisions. Information is displayed in the right time, in the format to make informed decisions.

Planning Considerations

ERP and CRM systems provide a broad range of features and functionality to support a wide variety of organizations. The designers of these applications have developed industry best practices based upon research and feedback. These enterprise applications integrate many functional areas normally controlled by legacy applications. Each disparate legacy application/data combination typically supports an individual functional area such as finance, ordering, logistics, human resources, etc. Only recently have organizations become aware of what the magnitude of the integrations cost, ranging from twenty to forty percent of organizational

IT budgets! Often it is the indirect or hidden costs that are difficult to predict.

These enterprise applications offer an assortment of modules that integrate seamlessly to provide specialized functionality for different types of organizations. Without a firm understanding of the business requirements and processes, the decision to purchase and configure the application can only be made based upon advertised descriptions along with the features and functionality of a particular module. A manager may summarily reject purchasing and implementing a module due to a lack of understanding of the value it can provide.

The challenge for the organization is to view the process from end to end rather than providing enhancements in one functional business area. The enterprise application can offer value-added functionality such as automation, workflow, reporting and consolidation of activities. The project team needs to address opportunities for improvement across many functional areas by leveraging the application's best practices and capabilities.

Validation of Outcomes
1. The selection of the enterprise application is based upon the current and near-term future requirements of the business and customers served.
2. A business case that includes a cost/benefit analysis showing the initial and ongoing operational costs.
3. A business capability assessment showing the ability of the organization to support the changes.
4. Current and future-state operational process maps that identify the areas for enhancement from the enterprise application.

Networks & Infrastructure

Build services that will support business demands and future growth.

This is performed at Level 2: Tactical.

Description

A network and infrastructure can be defined as the grouping of hardware devices and software components necessary to connect devices within the organization and to connect the organization to other organizations and the Internet.

- Typical hardware components utilized in a networking environment are network interface cards, computers, routers, hubs, switches, printers, and cabling and phone lines.
- Typical software components utilized in a networking environment are the network services and protocols needed to enable devices to communicate.

Only after the hardware is installed and configured can operating systems and software be installed into the network infrastructure. The operating systems which you install on your computers are considered the main software components within the network infrastructure. This is due to the operating system containing network communication protocols that enable network communication to occur. The operating system also typically includes applications and services that implement security for network communication.

Infrastructure-as-a-service (IaaS) systems are part of the cloud in which the IT infrastructure is deployed in a data center as a virtual machine. A virtual machine (VM) is a software implementation of a computer that executes programs like a physical machine. With IaaS clouds growing in popularity, tools and technologies are emerging that can transform an organization's existing infrastructure into a private or hybrid cloud.

125

Network security is a critical consideration within this activity. Network security refers to any activities designed to protect your network. Specifically, these activities protect the usability, reliability, integrity and safety of your data and network. Effective network security targets a variety of threats and stops them from entering or spreading on your network.

Desired Outcomes
- Select hardware and software components that are aligned to the technical architectural principles to meet future needs.
- Determine how to execute the virtualization approach and plans.
- Establish network security to protect the data without limiting or excluding user groups or data sources.
- The infrastructure is designed to support mobility.

Inputs
- A common understanding of the change vision in terms that can be implemented.
- Technical architectural principles are defined, understood and easily executed in support of the change.
- A well-defined future-state business process that identifies the network and infrastructure required to support the changes.
- An understanding of the data structures and sources along with the ability to ensure that the data is safe and secure.

Tools and Techniques
- Delivery vehicle overview planning
- Technology Infrastructure Release Guidelines
- Quality functional deployment
- Interviews and focus groups

Metrics
Infrastructure-centric effectiveness: The ability to measure the efficiency, speed and/or capacity of the technology:

- Throughput — amount of information that can pass through a system in a given amount of time.
- Transaction speed — speed at which a system can process a transaction.
- System availability — measured inversely as downtime, or the average amount of time a system is down or unavailable.
- Accuracy — measured inversely as error rate, or the number of errors per thousand/million that a system generates.
- Response time — average time to respond to a user-generated event, such as a mouse click.
- Scalability — conceptual metric related to how well a system can be adapted to increased demands.

Planning Considerations

Gather the requirements across the applications, business processes, people/organization, and information and knowledge management tracks when defining network infrastructure component requirements. Ensure that the business capability aspects which define the network and infrastructure are monitored and incorporated throughout development. The technical architects must identify and manage the risk areas throughout the planning and coordination of these tasks.

Validation of Outcomes

The network and infrastructure must align with and support the core values, change vision and the technical architectural principles to deliver the business requirements.

Technical Compliance

Implement and validate compliance requirements.

This is performed at Level 2: Tactical.

Description

Software has become a vital component to ensure the success of any business. This valuable asset must be accurately tracked and efficiently managed. Yet, very few organizations have an effective process for managing software assets. As organizations continue to grow, so do the number of software licenses and the IT budget dedicated to purchasing and managing those licenses.

Developing and maintaining an effective and efficient software compliance program is vital for the management of software, especially when large-scale change may dramatically alter how the software is used. Organizations must implement a solution that ensures compliance with current software license agreements and consistently monitor for potential violations. By effectively managing software licenses, companies can avoid paying penalties and dealing with possible legal issues while significantly cutting software licensing and maintenance costs. With the current regulatory environment, it causes corporate officers to be concerned with safeguarding against legal and financial exposure for regulatory non-compliance of software.

While compliance is usually the primary objective of organizations concerned about software license audits, or vendor billing, software optimization is the ultimate benefit. Organizations can use the resulting information to maximize the value of their software assets. Software is a huge cost for most organizations. Licensing of software can be complex, depending upon terms of use. As the organization becomes more virtual with cloud computing and mobile applications, it becomes a challenge to determine who is using the software and in what fashion are they using it to perform their jobs. Organizations tend to use only approximately seventy percent of the server licenses they pay for and only about seventy percent of capacity. According to leading analysts, many CIOs believe that as much as twenty percent of all installed desktop software is unused, often becoming "shelfware." Software optimization depends on knowing who is using what, how much and whether software is just running as opposed to being used in a meaningful way. Software license agreements should be evaluated and renegotiated to ensure that the organization is getting the best value.

Desired Outcomes
- Changes to the access and use of software are documented.
- Leverage software capabilities in an optimal way to ensure the greatest capacity.
- Conduct comprehensive software audits to ensure licensing compliance.
- Business continuity plans are updated to reflect the changes.

Inputs
- Current and future-state technical architecture identifies new, changing or outdated software, or a change in the number of users.
- The plans and design of the use of cloud computing.
- Changes within the organizational structure.

Tools and Techniques
- Software asset management audit process
- Risk assessments
- Surveys and interviews

Metrics
License compliance: The maximum concurrent use limit of either virtual or physical technologies for specific software.

Planning Considerations

Software licensing models are complex and constantly changing, making it difficult to manage. Many organizations are seeking a pay-per-use type of model that more directly aligns software application usage to the software licensing model. Organizations want to be in compliance, but find it difficult to manage this requirement. Here are some additional considerations that will support this task:

- IT organizations need to monitor and track software usage over time, not just during an audit where it provides a snapshot in time.
- Software compliance and maintenance metrics need to be established along with measures that align to the software licensing requirements, contracts and conditions.
- Major change initiatives that impact the organizational structure, staffing levels, business processes, virtualization, mobility and other interactions that impact software usability should be assessed.
- Software auditing and asset management tools should be considered to ensure compliance.

Validation of Outcomes

1. Software requirements and usage is mapped to the change initiative.
2. A comprehensive audit is conducted to identify software assets and usage.
3. Software metrics and measures are in place.
4. Business continuity and disaster recovery plans are updated based upon the changes and updated findings.

Application Functions/Modules

Configure the application to enhance business processes incorporating best practices.

This is performed at Level 3: Operational.

Description

Enterprise software applications offer a great deal of functional enhancements to processes within business operations. Software vendors incorporate business best practices into their design along with offering modular functionality allowing semi-customizable application of their systems. These modular features save both time and money by enhancing the business without changing the software's source code. Integration capabilities allow functional business operations share required information to create a near seamless flow of information from end-to-end. Enterprise Resource Planning (ERP) systems aid in integrating and often automating back office operations like procurement, human resources management, pay and benefits administration, accounts payable, accounts receivable, asset management, etc. Other enterprise systems such as Customer Resource Management (CRM) provide integration and automation to the front office operations. Sales, customer service, technical support centers, partner channel management as well as other business areas have customer information readily available to allow employees to make informed decisions.

From a tactical perspective, the integration of these systems not only enhances the performance of the process from end to end, but significantly reduces operational cost. At an operational level, the features and functionality of specific ERP and CRM modules further enhance the work activities by automating administrative tasks, providing workflow, and reducing many of the administrative tasks. The functionality that these integrated modules provide will create a fundamental shift from administrative duties to a customer-focused, problem-solving and decision-making role.

Delivering value at each stage of the business process is enhanced by technology. However, process improvement comes at a cost that needs to be evaluated and weighed to determine overall value. Adding technology to the process can be expensive; there is an initial cost followed by ongoing maintenance and licensing fees. Technology can also add an extra layer of complexity to the business in terms of support, training, integration and maintenance. A careful evaluation should be performed to determine if the technology is replacing the personal customer service touch that may be a key differentiator for the business. An automated telephone answering service is an example where technology improved the process, but some could argue that it diminished customer service.

Desired Outcomes
Operational-level features and functionality in the software application have been identified to provide value in process improvements.

Inputs
A clear understanding of business requirements and the detailed business processes in which value is delivered to the customer.

Tools and Techniques
- Application requirements definition and guidelines
- Quality functional deployment
- Task analysis
- User analysis

Metrics
Value to Cost Ratio: Evaluates the actual and potential value that is being delivered to the customers compared to the cost associated with creating that value.

Complexity Reduction: Determines the reduction of the level of complexity within the business by enabling technology within the process.

Business Operation Impact: Appraise the impact on the organization due to the change in terms of time, cost and quality.

Planning Considerations

At the operational level of detail, the activities and tasks are analyzed for performance and efficiency within the business process. Additional requirements are gathered from appropriate stakeholders. The requirements are then identified and integrated into the process where the features and functionality is fully leveraged from the application. Analysis can run concurrent with requirements gathering. Analysis should start as soon as sufficient information about the future requirements is available. The project team should treat the quality requirements differently from the functional requirements.

When defining requirements, plan for increased complexity when the user base is extended to discretionary users, customers, suppliers and end users. Keep in mind these users will have a different perspective on how they may interact with the process and the associated software applications. The requirements of the application functionality should reflect the needs of the target audience, especially when usability and functional requirements differ. When designing applications that extend beyond the organization, the focus should be on delivering rich types of content, but with an increased focus on security controls. Because business needs can change significantly, consider using business scenarios as a technique for driving out functional requirements and addressing variability issues.

Validation of Outcomes

1. Operational requirements are satisfied in the design of the application.
2. Performance and efficiency within the process have been identified.

Mobility and Accessibility

Provide access to systems and information based upon business needs.

This is performed at Level 3: Operational.

Description

Enterprise mobility enables a workforce to have instant access to information through mobile applications, anywhere and anytime. Employees have been fundamentally changing the way they work, and in order to remain competitive, organizations are making enterprise applications accessible through mobile devices.

By allowing mobile, instant communication and access to important information to the workforce, enterprise mobility improves productivity by providing the information the moment it is needed. With the continual increase of organizations utilizing mobile applications to improve customer responsiveness and worker productivity, it is essential to evolve the business into the next generation of technology usage to respond to evolving customer requirements.

Frequently, companies require increased mobility to get close to their customers, able to respond quickly before their competition takes the advantage. To achieve mobility, equipment must be purchased to meet the current and future needs and functionality. Likewise, connectivity to enterprise applications is needed to maintain access to information and near real time functionality, especially the ability to update customer information.

Enterprise mobility brings with it the convenience of size from a handheld device, as well as the savings from cost. Companies that use enterprise mobility also frequently see a significant return on investment from having the information they need when they need it, which can at many times provide the competitive edge for sales and marketing teams. Mobile devices can also integrate with cloud-hosted services such as

Exchange Online, which provides users with the ability to respond to schedule changes and new e-mails on the fly. When decision makers are able to communicate approvals to employees, regardless of location, tasks can get done quickly and efficiently.

Desired Outcomes
Provide enterprise mobility and access to information to conduct business in a cost effective manner.

Inputs
Identify the requirements to perform business operations remotely by using mobile devices and specific information. Business processes are defined to work remotely and security provides safe access to the information.

Tools and Techniques
- Cost/benefit analysis
- Option engineering
- Impact analysis
- Process modeling

Metrics
Enterprise mobile operations: Mobile functionality provides timely and in-depth information to conduct business in an efficient and cost effective manner.

Planning Considerations
Whether employees conduct meetings across the country or down the street at a local coffee shop, the ability to remotely access and connect to enterprise services is not only advantageous for your productivity, but also for the overall well-being of your organization.

Giving employees the option to work from home, or remote-in when away on business, makes for a happier, more productive staff. As technology continues to advance, mobile devices like tablets, laptops and even smartphones are making it easier to conduct business. The idea is not to move all of the staff out of the office; rather, the concept is to create an alternative way of working that connects employees with customers no matter where they are located.

While mobile devices are extremely beneficial in enterprise mobility, they aren't the only way to take advantage of enterprise mobility. Software applications via the Web are also beneficial to creating accessibility outside of the office.

The major concern for any mobile application is the accessibility to sensitive information and the security controls. Accessibility should not be restricted just because the user is remote. This thinking diminishes the service levels and performance of the process. Rather, security controls should be instituted that ensure the protection of the information and intellectual capital.

Validation of Outcomes
1. A cost/benefit analysis is performed to determine the value of the mobility services and equipment.
2. Remote users have remote access to information to perform their jobs efficient and effectively.
3. Security controls are put into place to protect, rather than control the information and intellectual capital.
4. Mobile equipment is user-friendly and has the ability to access enterprise applications.

Technical Support

Develop processes and resources to meet the needs of the business during transformational change.

This is performed at Level 3: Operational.

Description

Technical support provides a wide range of services and supports a level of expertise that guides and trains users. Technical support assists in solving complex technical problems that employees face when working in the business world. To effectively manage resources, technical support can be provided in a tiered service model. Although there are differing approaches, it generally is provided this way: Tier 0 is provided by local subject matter experts; Tier 1 provides online documentation; Tier 2 offers telephone support from a trained technician; Tier 3 provides remote access of the computer to repair or configure an application; and Tier 4 offers on-site repair service of the computer. The technical support team can be offered on-site, from an off-shore location, or provided by a third-party contractor. Each offering provides advantages and also disadvantages. The primary consideration must be to provide ongoing support to users — whether they are employees, contractors, suppliers or customers. This service offering must be able to effectively resolve problems, provide guidance and answer questions of these users. This means that whenever the user is conducting business and runs into problems, the technical support services must be available to ensure current service levels, performance and customer satisfaction.

During a large-scale change, technical support becomes the critical link to support the business. The business and IT must be capable of supporting the current business operations and an interim or transitional state, while developing a future state. These three conditions can create an increase in complexity as well as a drain in resources. The technical support team needs not only to be aware, but have a level of understanding of the changes in the systems, networks and applications that support the changing processes and work activities. It becomes a challenge to determine the true cause of an issue: Is the problem a bug in the software, an error in configuration, a user not trained correctly, or a process or procedural issue that needs to be corrected. Many times, the issue could be caused by multiple problems. The project team needs to make available a wide range of documents to the technical support group and keep them apprised of the changes. In addition, the technical support center needs to coordinate with the business to be able to address issues or questions that may not be technical in nature.

Desired Outcomes
The technical support center is capable of supporting the current business operations, while understanding the changes in an interim or transitional state to support the business users (employees, suppliers and customers) without diminishing service levels or performance.

Inputs
- Understanding of the operation and functionality of current systems.
- Changes in the business processes and technical systems.
- Understanding of the interim business operations and applications.
- Current service levels and KPIs.

Tools and Techniques
- Documented processes and procedures.
- Coordinate with the project team and business to resolve issues quickly.
- Monitor service levels and performance metrics using a dashboard.
- Anticipate increase workload/call volume and staff accordingly.
- Contingency plans.

Metrics
Technical service levels: Systems, including applications, networks and databases, are operating as designed and functioning at prescribed levels.

Operational service levels: Business operational task issues are identified and handled separately from technical issues.

Planning Considerations

The initiative can create several changes in the way in which a system operates and interacts with other systems. As a result, the technical support center staff will need to be trained on new functionality, applications and other systems that have changed as a result of the transformation. Depending upon the situation, a new or specialized group within the support staff may need to be assigned to handle the change. In some cases, the level of expertise required for support may call for new technical staff to be hired rather than training the existing staff. During the change initiative, there is a learning curve that takes place for the users and support staff. The adoption of new practices may create a decrease in operational performance, quality and service levels. Staffing levels in the support center may need to be adjusted to accommodate for this transition period. During the transitional period, applications, networks, interfaces and databases may not function as desired, resulting in operational problems in other areas of the business. Increased processing demand of the new systems may create performance problems on the network. These issues may not be anticipated, requiring a contingency plan to mitigate the problem.

Validation of Outcomes

1. Staffing levels at the technical support center are adjusted to meet the anticipated demand.
2. Contingency plans are developed to mitigate risk to sustain the current service levels and performance.

Application Configuration

Configure the application to meet the unique business requirements.

This is performed at Level 4: Functional.

Description

Enterprise software vendors design their applications with industry best practices into add-on modules. There are a variety of features and functionality that are bundled into the application that should be investigated to determine if they are appropriate for the business. To determine which capabilities to leverage, future-state business processes need to be mapped at the functional level. Examination of the business process should reveal areas where improvements or enhancements should be made. Once the new functionality has been defined, it should be incorporated into the process. However, implementing best practices may change the current business processes, work tasks and reporting.

There are characteristics inherent within information that can be used to problem-solve and make decisions. As the data from various sources is integrated within the enterprise application, defining the attributes becomes extremely critical to be able to classify, define and sort the information correctly.

The proper configuration of enterprise software is critical to the effective operation of the business. Defining the data attributes within the fields on the pages is crucial to ensure collaboration, integration, and coordination of processes and systems.

Desired Outcomes

Business best practices are applied using enterprise applications by installing and configuring modules and defining the attributes of the data.

Inputs
- Knowledge of enterprise application features and functionality
- Future-state business processes
- Detailed business requirements and compliance

Tools and Techniques
- Collaborative work sessions (between IT and the business)
- Requirements review and assessment
- Gap analysis and gap closure of business processes
- Analysis of data and data sources

Metrics
Functionality alignment: The features and functionality offered in enterprise applications provide measurable value to the business process.

Planning Considerations
The project team must have a strong understanding of the gap between the current and future-state processes, along with an understanding of out-of-the-box functionality of the capabilities found within the enterprise application. A major challenge of the team is to understand the changes in the business processes that will be driven by the application. These changes may include automating key activities and workflow for approval authorization, to name a few. These changes may shift tasks once performed by one role or group to another. The change may require an increase in responsibility or the need to learn a new skill set to adequately accomplish the task. Shifting responsibilities and tasks can bring about fear, resentment, confusion and frustration, if the objectives are not fully communicated.

Out-of-the-box functionality means that the source code is not changed in any way. This may require the business to do things somewhat differently while achieving the same outcome. In many cases, these changes may appear to limit activities, or force actions that appear to be different or new. These changes should be accommodated rather than to seek a custom coding solution that could be quite costly and limit long-term functionality or support.

When disparate systems and data sources are brought together, there is often a wide range of attributes that need to be standardized into a common list. The challenge for developers is to create a folksonomy, or in other words, a common language that users will recognize and understand. Users need to ensure that the meaning of a word or phrase is consistent across the organization. Everyone should have a common reference model to work from to describe the management of the information within the process.

Validation of Outcomes

1. Business best practices though the uses of add-on application modules are incorporated to enhance the business process.
2. Out-of-the-box functionality of enterprise applications is used rather than custom coding.
3. Employees understand the changes in business process and work steps that are driven by the out-of-the-box functionality.
4. A common language or folksonomy is utilized and understood by all members throughout the enterprise.
5. Data attributes are standardized to limit the complexity.

Interfaces

Link applications and databases in order to share information.

This is performed at Level 4: Functional.

Description

An interface is an interconnection between two or more systems that allows the exchange of information. An interface can also be an interconnection between applications and the users. The primary purpose of an interface is to be able to interact with the systems to effectively leverage the information. Interface design principles need to be developed and followed in order to meet user requirements. In the past, computer software was designed with little regard for the user, so the user had to somehow adapt to the system. This approach to system design is not at all appropriate today; the system must adapt to the user. This is why design principles are so important.

An interface design team, in conjunction with managers, team leaders and workers, should figure out together which principles are the most appropriate for their environment and work tasks. They should then focus on purchasing or developing software products with usable and productive interfaces to exemplify those key principles. Here are some common key principles:

- Designers need to first understand the users, their needs and the objectives in order to create an interface that allows them to effectively access the system's functionality.
- With more applications moving to the cloud and the browser becoming our operating system, creating effective, easy and enjoyable interfaces for our web products has never been more important. Designers need to create a web interface that is user-friendly and familiar to those migrating from desktop programs.

- Create a consistent look and feel to system interfaces that allow the actions performed by users to meet the expected outcomes. If the same action is repeated, the system needs to respond in a consistent manner.
- A good way to test the interface design is by watching people use the system in a real-world scenario. The users should be able to easily navigate around the application and achieve their objectives with relative ease. In addition, the interface should be intuitive to both experienced and less-experienced computer users.

Desired Outcomes
Interfaces are created to meet user needs that are easy to navigate and consistent.

Inputs
Understanding the user and business requirements prior to designing user interfaces.

Tools and Techniques
- Interviews and focus groups
- Develop and use key design principles
- Simulations: low- and high-fidelity testing
- Wireframes
- Process mapping — work steps

Metrics
Interface usability: Interfaces are designed to provide ease of use and consistency across all systems.

Planning Considerations
Work steps are often performed in a specific sequence using applications to aid in its facilitation. Developers need to understand this work sequence and develop a user interface that would emulate that sequence without the user jumping to various pages or tabs.

In order to achieve an effective interface design, the use of wireframes during the design phase has become a valued method. A wireframe is a visual representation of the projected content and structure of a graphical user interface and is an essential step on the way to meeting the needs of the user. Testing the wireframe requires the user to indicate where they would most likely find specific fields or action buttons. Collecting feedback from a sample group of users allows designers to identify the most appropriate layout to create an efficient application. The paper diagram is easily understood by all stakeholders and can serve as a communication aid. Much like an architect's blueprint plans, wireframes are an invaluable tool as a first step in the design. This technique is often called low-fidelity testing.

Once the low-fidelity design has been confirmed, high-fidelity prototypes are created very close to the true representation of the final user interface design. This mock-up provides valuable information about the user's perception of the application's look and feel. The prototype shows users drop down menus, radio buttons, color scheme, pop-up messages and workflow logic. The high-fidelity prototype is the final test of the layout and the usability functionality.

A final consideration should be for users with special needs, such as visual impairments or colorblindness. Provisions should be made that meet these special requirements.

Validation of Outcomes
1. The design of the user interface meets user requirements in terms of layout, functionality, workflow and color selection.
2. The look and feel should be consistent with other applications.

Functional Parameters

Define the type of data and naming convention to standardize the task.

This is performed at Level 4: Functional.

Description

A functional parameter in a software application is the choice of variables for a particular function. Selecting an employment type is the function, and the parameters are the status type, such as full-time, part-time, seasonal, temporary or student intern. Depending upon the design, each parameter may include or exclude specific functionality. A part-time employment status may not trigger access to benefits. Standardizing functional parameters is critical, especially when multiple sources are integrated into a single database. When separate business units that use similar information are combined, it is important to agree on a standard term and function that would apply across the enterprise to reduce complexity. A full-time employee at business unit "A" may define this status as having assigned work of 32 hours or more per week, whereas business unit "B" may define this status of having assigned work of 40 hours per week. When these situations arise, the process and policies become standardized, or the naming convention for the parameter should change to identify the different standard. In this case, the parameters should indicate FT-32 (full-time — 32 hours) and FT-40 (full-time — 40 hours), respectively.

In some applications, the data type and field length are fixed. Data types may be limited to alpha characters, alpha-numeric characters, or strictly numeric characters. The folksonomy (common terminology) should be defined and shared throughout the organization. The full-time hours abbreviation is an example of the folksonomy used in the application (FT-32 and FT-40). With this example, the term "FT" indicates "full-time." The term "FT-32" may indicate that an employee designated full-time may have that status with "32" hours assigned, whereas, another employee may have the full-time designation if they are assigned "40" hours. The rules, standards or policies would govern the use of that status.

There may be many functional parameters created due to the constraints of the system, due to the data type. As a result, these new parameters need to be defined and standardized across the organization. These new parameter terms will become part of the new folksonomy. Careful consideration should be given to the parameters if multiple languages are used. The meaning could change from one language to another, creating confusion.

Desired Outcomes
Functional parameters should be standardized, where possible, to reduce the level of complexity. Common terminology should be used to maintain a shared level of understanding.

Inputs
- Understanding of data types used within the application.
- Standardized business processes, especially when multiple organizations or business units are involved.
- Business rules and detailed business requirements.
- Data sources — clean and accurate data.

Tools and Techniques
- Interviews and focus groups
- Future-state business process reviews and standardization
- Data cleansing
- Application functionality review (ID data types for fields)

Metrics
Standardized functional parameters: Data parameters are standardized to reduce the level of complexity. The organization has a common understanding of the terminology of the parameters.

Planning Considerations

The data type for a particular field can be defined in some applications, while some fields are pre-defined, depending upon the application. In addition to the data-type requirements, the field length is fixed. Each data element must be clarified and defined with the business users. Once the requirements are defined and understood, then the data elements need to be cleansed.

Data cleansing, also known as data scrubbing, is the process of ensuring that a set of data is correct and accurate. During this process, records are checked for accuracy and consistency, and they are either corrected or deleted as necessary. This can occur within a single set of records or between multiple sets of data that need to be merged or that will work together.

Validation of Outcomes

1. Like or similar work tasks are standardized between business units or other functional areas.
2. A common naming convention is used and understood by the organization.
3. Parameter descriptions reflect the data-type format used for the particular field within the application.
4. Data is cleansed and ready to use.

Performance Driver Track: Information and Knowledge Management

The Change Champion – Knowledge Management

Lead and direct the knowledge management track.

This is performed at Level 1: Strategy.

Description

One of the most significant tasks to winning the game is the change champion. The change champion is an inspiring leader who turns the vision into action. The task of the change champion is to use his or her leadership skills to guide and direct the activities in the information and knowledge management track of work. This starts by thinking in new and unique ways to execute the vision in terms of the value that is provided and enhanced through the philosophies, methodology, approach and frameworks that will support the management of knowledge used in the change initiative. Simply stated, how will the employees identify, interpret and use the individual and collective knowledge to provide value to the change initiative and the organization.

The goal is to provide the right information, at the right time, in the right format to employees so they can make informed decisions. In addition, the lessons learned from past experiences or the collective knowledge is captured and used to improve the quality of those decisions. The challenge is to identify knowledge from the vast amount of information that resides within individuals and work groups throughout the organization. This is called tribal knowledge and is often unwritten information that is unknown to others outside of the group. It is assumed to be factual, but has no known data or analysis to verify that it is accurate. The information is often gained from experiences that when acted upon are supported and accepted by others within the organization. The knowledge is gained through observation, information, education, skills and experiences that are supported by others and accepted. Knowledge management, therefore, is the discipline that enables individuals, teams and organizations to collectively gather, evaluate, store and share knowledge throughout the organization.

The benefits to the organization can be highly strategic and transformational, as well as operational. There are many new technologies including Web 2.0, social networking and blogs that help us communicate, collaborate and learn in unique and, possibly, disruptive ways. These new tools can challenge traditional strategies in their design and use of new technologies, access and control of information, and the development and management of employees. Organizations are rapidly evolving from a global organization to now include the global individual as the knowledge worker.

Desired Outcomes
The organization enables leveraging the knowledge and, in turn, improves efficiency and effectiveness by creating, transferring and applying knowledge.

Inputs
Understand the organization's core values, culture, and guiding principles that will influence employee behavior. Understand the internal and external influencers that drive the change.

Tools and Techniques
- Business simulation
- Content analysis
- Learning networks
- Cross-functional teams
- After-action reviews
- Expertise profiling
- Knowledge mapping
- Organizational culture assessment/alignment

Metrics

Mission success rate. This metric is calculated by the percentage of tasks in the track of work that succeeded to meet their desired outcomes divided by the number of tasks.

Planning Considerations

The change champion of the information and knowledge management track needs to understand the principles, methods and operational requirements consistent with the need to leverage information into knowledge and wisdom within the organization to remain competitive. In addition, there are specific characteristics that each change champion should possess. These character traits are not as much about specific competencies of knowledge management frameworks, business intelligence, content management system or social networking, but rather focus on leading employees to carry out their assigned tasks in order to complete the project's mission within a specific timeframe and achieve the desired outcomes.

Knowledge management may not be totally understood within organizations. Knowledge management is a management approach which incorporates cultural, business processes and supportive technical infrastructures for intelligent extraction of knowledge throughout the organization. It also serves to enable the creation of new knowledge in order to meet and support the organizational vision and the organization's business objectives. It has two main purposes: assist the organization to be more effective, such as to create value, and also aid the organization to act more efficient, to increase both financial and knowledge capital.

Knowledge management is not a technical system, nor should the role be technical in nature. However, technology can enable the creation of knowledge throughout the organization. Some organizations believe that business intelligence and knowledge management are one in the same. Business intelligence specialists work with applications and databases to provide reporting and analytic tools to allow employees to make informed decisions. Fundamentally, business intelligence and knowledge management have the same objective — to focus on improving business performance. However, the purpose of knowledge management is to achieve the maximum degree of understanding of one's operating environment and relevant circumstances that can advance or retard progress toward an objective.

Listed in Appendix B is an evaluation assessment that is used to select and assess the change champion. This assessment evaluates twenty leadership characteristics needed for this role. The specific function of the technology change champion is to address the end-to-end workflow defined in the change initiative to meet customer and business requirements. Simply put, the role is developed to guide the fundamental rethinking and redesign of business operations to achieve dramatic improvements in critical measures of performance, such as cost, quality, service and speed, to add value for the customer and the business.

Validation of Outcomes

1. Were there frequent and honest discussions with the team members about the potential threats and an examination of the opportunities that should be taken?
2. Did the change champion describe the change vision in terms that could be easily understood and acted upon?
3. Was there an emotional commitment among the project team track that built a strong team coalition with support and guidance from the change champion?
4. Were obstacles identified and removed, allowing the project team to perform their task efficiently and effectively?
5. Were there defined goals and measures in place and clearly understood by project team members performing each key task?

Taxonomy and Folksonomy of Content

Develop the methodology to classify content, build naming conventions, and categorize data.

This is performed at Level 1: Strategy.

Description

Most enterprises agree that knowledge is an essential asset for success and survival within an increasingly competitive and global market. Therefore, taxonomies and folksonomies are developed to manage their information. Taxonomy is a classification system that is used to group things according to their similarities in some respect, such as similarities in structure, role, behavior, etc. The challenge of knowledge management is one of context — understanding the user's frame of reference, mental model, problem-solving approach and stage of process in their work task. We also want to know something about how people describe the things they require and their understanding of labels that are placed on documents. All of this information points to the requisite for terminology that is consistent, and multiple facets that can be used to describe the various attributes of content; in other words, a taxonomy. As organizations attempt to deal with the abundance of information, managers are recognizing the need for organizing principles that can extend across organizational silos, span the enterprise, and connect disparate systems and repositories. Taxonomies and other categorization schemes offer solutions that can provide a structure to effectively manage the overload of information.

However, the formal structures or taxonomy that an organization uses to find information may not be understood or work effectively for everyone. Therefore, a collaborative tagging system called folksonomy is also used as a means to label pieces of information such as photographs, web pages, documents and web links. This form of classification became popular on the Web around 2004 as part of social networking applications. Tagging, which is one of the defining characteristics of Web

153

2.0 services, allows users to collectively classify and find information. Some websites include tag clouds as a way to visualize tags in a folksonomy. An example of this can be found on smartphones with user-defined cloud tags used to point out good restaurants or points of interest.

Used together, taxonomies and folksonomies can provide a common understanding and a shared vocabulary to identify, search and group a mass amount of complex information that can be synthesized into usable knowledge. However, this can only be accomplished through the adoption of technical architectural principles that support social networking and cloud computing; business processes that leverage technology in a way that allows employees to focus delivering value to their customers; and creating an organizational culture that is adaptive to change and encourages employees to do their best and share information.

Desired Outcomes
Create a structure to enable the users to identify, classify and categorize information that can be turned into knowledge.

Inputs
An organizational culture that supports collaboration in their core values as a way to share information and knowledge to support the vision and goals of the organization.

Define technical architecture principles that will enable the sharing of information through the use of mobile and cloud computing systems.

Tools and Techniques
1. Content Management Systems (CMS) such as SharePoint
2. Metadata software
3. Social networking
4. Access to information via cloud computing

Metrics

The percentage of practices fulfilled: The ability of the organization to follow policies, practices and standards that eliminate ambiguity and redundancy, and control the vocabulary defined by the taxonomy.

Planning Considerations

One of the biggest challenges in the management of knowledge and content, whether it exists in papers, books or from a database, has been to create a method to organize and mark the information in such a way that it can be found again when the need arises. The practice of tagging and the building of folksonomies is being used as a way to allow any content creator or content user to organize and label knowledge in a way that makes sense to them. Over time, a group of users/creators may build a type of taxonomy that is intuitive to them and easy to apply. There are few hierarchical relationships to deal with, no attempting to match a predetermined term to a piece of information that may not quite fit. Folksonomies are a joint venture that is extremely immediate and responsive to a user base. However, tagging without a common base of understanding can quickly become unworkable. There is a lot of ambiguity inherent in this type of system since the same word or tag may not mean the same to each member of a group. Eventually, the folksonomy starts to resemble and be treated as a taxonomy with the rules of usage that tagging and folksonomies tend to avoid.

Validation of Outcomes
1. Processes and procedures are defined to govern the taxonomy.
2. Structure, membership and accountabilities are created.
3. Practices, standards and measures are established to determine how the taxonomy and folksonomy will be monitored and controlled.
4. Technical and business architecture is designed to support the taxonomy and folksonomy.

Social Networking Philosophy and Strategy

Crate a method of augmenting official channels of communication to connect with customers.

This is performed at Level 1: Strategy.

Description

The social networking philosophy is a set of beliefs and principles on how the organization interacts with and collaborates with their employees, customers and the public at large. These concepts should align with the core values of the organization and is reflected in the organization's culture. The social networking strategy should explicitly address how the social media and social networking processes and technologies can be applied to the organizational operations in order to help it achieve its goals.

Social networking strategy development begins with identifying the goals of the organization. These goals drive the organization's planning and operational efforts in areas such as sales, marketing, public relations, customer service and product development. Goal identification requires working with top management to identify key strategic goals, along with the associated metrics the organization uses to tell whether or not the organization is meeting those goals.

The business advantages and benefits of social networking in the workplace are still very much underappreciated and undervalued by some leaders. Although some organizations have started to implement some of the facets of social networking technology and reap the business benefits, fear, resistance and risk are the opinions that still dominate many organizations. Creating a social media strategy is a complex endeavor because it fundamentally changes the way in which the organization defines requirements for products and services, markets target customers, shares information and determines the proper degree of engagement outside the organization.

Desired Outcomes

Develop a social networking strategy that is consistent with and aligns to the core values and vision of the organization by becoming more responsive to people/consumer audiences; incorporating customer and audience feedback into the organization to be more responsive; humanizing the company's brand; and increasing the awareness and strength of the organization's products and services by providing clear and accurate information.

Inputs

An organizational culture that supports collaboration in their core values as a way to share information and knowledge to support the vision and goals of the organization.

The technical architectural principles and systems are aligned and support the social networking philosophy.

Tools and Techniques
- Interviews and focus groups
- Business case development
- Strategic roadmaps
- Review of technical architectural principles and strategy
- Organizational culture assessment and alignment

Metrics

The effectiveness of service levels: The ability of the organization to solve the customer problem through the interaction of social media.

Case and call deflection: The percent of change in call volume by responding to customer inquiries and issues in a timely manner and providing the appropriate level of information needed that will satisfy the customer needs.

Planning Considerations

Organizations need to better understand social networking and its benefits, as well as its potential detriments. Social networking changes the rules on how organizations relate to their customers. It is a fundamental shift from a customer focused approach, where products and services are provided to the customer, to a customer centric approach where the customer is part of the process.

Customers provide instant feedback on how they feel about the products or services as well as their feeling about the company. Organizations have to be prepared to respond quickly to the requests, allowing them to become transparent. Messages, once generated from corporate communications, or the marketing department to customers now may come from all parts of the organization and at all levels. Attempts to limit the source to "official" information is naive since in reality, informal information is going on by employees, former employees, customers, suppliers, and competitors. Rather than restricting communication, the focus should foster a culture of trust, support, and empowerment. A happy and satisfied employee will be a great advocate of the company, products and services to the public than any marketing campaign could achieve.

Validation of Outcomes
1. The social networking philosophy and strategy is a written document that describes how the core values of the organization align and support social networking.
2. The business case indicates the return on investment from social networking opportunities.
3. A constructive and adaptive organizational culture promotes employee and customer satisfaction.
4. Policies on communicating with the public are changed to support and align with a social networking approach.

Knowledge Management Framework

Develop the principles and rules to capture and develop knowledge within the organization.

This is performed at Level 1: Strategy.

Description:

A knowledge management framework is an integrated system that includes roles and accountabilities, processes, technologies, and governance that the organization puts into place to maximize the value and application of the organization's knowledge. It will provide a managed approach to building, developing, and retaining know-how in service of business goals through wisdom obtained through this system.

- KM People - Organization: Knowledge management roles have to be established in the business, communities need to be set up to share and reuse tacit knowledge, behaviors such as seeking and sharing knowledge need to be incentivized, and to become the accepted way to work.
- KM Processes: There has to be a tried-and-tested process for capturing, distilling, validating, storing, applying and reusing knowledge, and also for innovation of new concepts.
- KM Technologies: The people and the process need to be supported by enabling technologies, which allows knowledge to be found and accessed wherever it resides (in databases, on the Intranet, in people's heads). IT plays an important role in KM, by providing the technology to allow people to communicate and share information.
- KM Governance: Controls are used in the technical systems to manage versions of documents, to define and categorize information, and to authorize how the information is managed.

The information gathered from these integrated systems is in the form of explicit knowledge where the information can be articulated, codified, and stored in a document management system, a learning management system, or other such repositories. This information is readily known knowledge that can be shared among members of the organization for training, standardization of work practices, or for reporting purposes.

The true power of the knowledge management framework is the ability to bring seemingly unrelated information together from the existing documents and data to realize patterns of behavior, or characteristics that were once undiscovered. This knowledge may not be readily apparent but rather through experience or intuition where new knowledge is discovered. Due to our preconceptions of how we were taught to perform a task, we naturally reject ways that do not make sense, or run counter to what we have learned and know to be true. However, introducing concepts from other disciplines, or combining seeming disparate pieces of data, the user may discover knowledge that can be applied to the business that can create a competitive advantage.

Desired Outcomes
To create a structure where information can be collected, sorted, managed, analyzed, and used to share and create knowledge.

Inputs
The organizational culture should support the sharing and contribution of information. Employee's performance measurement plans are designed in part to promote content submission and thought leadership. The technical architectural principles support a knowledge network.

Tools and Techniques
- Create rewards and other incentives
- Develop and document knowledge management processes
- Knowledge Mapping
- After action reviews
- Develop taxonomy and folksonomy of information

Metrics

Structured information to create knowledge outcomes: Creating the knowledge process, enhanced by the technologies, and supported by the organization to create knowledge as a measured value.

Planning Considerations

There is an English saying: "Two heads are better than one." This proverb stresses the importance of having a second person involved in whatever task one is performing. By having two people working together on one task, the job will be performed faster. If one person is an expert in a field that the other is not, then, the combining of expertise will make the job easier and smoother to run, thus ensuring the best results for the job. To achieve this collaborative work environment, the organization must create a culture of learning and support. This is achieved through supporting its core principles enforced through policies, leadership practices, and a flat organizational structure that empowers the workforce. Rewards and other incentives are used to contribute knowledge.

A well-defined process is needed to support how the knowledge is articulated, codified, and stored within the content or knowledge management system to support the organization. Metrics and measures can be used to monitor the effectiveness of the knowledge process.

Companies often use web-based content management systems (CMS) to manage knowledge-based processes and sites. However, CMS applications are not designed for knowledge management and because of several critical gaps in capabilities, many organizations are failing in their efforts to foster greater collaboration. Content and knowledge management systems are not the same. There are a several fundamental differences between a typical CMS and a KMS, specifically with regard to how information flows through development and publishing processes.

There are three components that support a knowledge management framework: 1) a knowledge resources component that characterizes knowledge resources that need to be managed; 2) an activities

161

component that identifies and explains the activities involved in manipulating these knowledge resources, and 3) the knowledge management influence component that recognize the factors that influence the conduct of knowledge management.

The KM resources component is comprised of three main types of resources: material, human and monetary. Each type of resource can affect each of the other resources as well as the external environment. These can be further divided to include participant's knowledge, organizational culture, and infrastructure.

The activities components include knowledge acquisition, knowledge selection, internalization of knowledge, and using knowledge. These are considered the starting point for the management of the knowledge.

The influence component is comprised of six factors that includes resources, leadership, managerial, coordination, measurement, and environmental. These influencers define the nature and outcome of the knowledge work.

Validation of Outcomes
1. A knowledge management framework is created and documented.
2. A framework of taxonomy and folksonomy of information is created.

Knowledge Development

Create the work environment and align the systems to develop and manage knowledge.

This is performed at Level 2: Tactical.

Description

Many organizations believe that their employees who possess the knowledge create documents which are then stored in their content management system, resulting in knowledge development. However, the documentation of information does not constitute organizational knowledge because the presumption is that other employees will read and understand the material, then apply the ideas, and concepts in the organization to enhance the value delivered to their customers.

Knowledge creation is more than sharing information, although socialization is a part of the process. First we need to better understand the meaning of knowledge and how it differs from information or wisdom. Information refers to data that has been given some meaning by way of a relational connection. Knowledge is the concise and appropriate collection of information in a way that makes it useful. Wisdom, on the other hand, refers to the ability to make sensible decisions and give good advice because of the experience and knowledge that a person has gained through explicit and tacit knowledge. Simply stated, explicit knowledge can be easily described whereas tacit information is more a feeling or emotion based upon their experiences.

Organizational knowledge is created in part through the ability of employees to socialize and share an understanding of the subject through a combination of education and experience. This is produced through the development of an adaptive and constructive culture where employees become a valued member of high-performing teams and where the physical work environment promotes close interaction with other members. Employees are encouraged and supported to achieve professional and organizational goals. Knowledge is gained through conversations, observation, mentoring and apprenticeships by sharing experiences, thoughts, and beliefs.

Knowledge is also gained through the ability to access information contained in knowledge management systems, content management systems, and web surfing. Using analytic tools, models, reports, and other business intelligence tools can provide insights to effectively problem-solve, and make informed decisions based upon the knowledge of the employees.

Desired Outcomes
Create a work environment and align systems that foster the exchange of information that creates organizational knowledge.

Inputs
Defining and supporting core values that will drive behaviors that will align to the knowledge development activities.

Create consistency of information structure and the common understanding of the terminology used within the organization.

Develop systems and structures that enable and promote the exchange of information within and between organizational units and the public.

Tools and Techniques
- Organizational culture assessment and alignment
- Mentoring, internships, and coaching
- Physical work environment design
- Interviews and focus groups

Metrics
Understanding and measurement: To gain a perspective on the evolution of knowledge within the organization.

Planning Considerations

To create an environment that promotes knowledge development first requires an organizational culture that fosters individual growth and development of individual employees while balancing the requirement to complete tasks within performance and quality standards.

A physical work environment promotes the exchange of information and interaction of employees. Remove high cubical walls that tend to isolate employees. Create an environment that supports socialization where employees can talk freely and share thoughts and ideas.

The organization should develop mentorship programs to develop the knowledge and skills of new or inexperienced employees. Collaborative career and performance goals with regularly scheduled feedback are used to encourage and support individuals. Formalized training programs and job aids are used to level set employees.

Knowledge management and content management systems are used to capture, store, codify, and access information. Analytic and reporting tools are used to aid in problem-solving and decision making.

Validation of Outcomes
1. Employees work collaboratively, sharing information and ideas. Employees are mentored and coached to develop their skills and knowledge.
2. Information can be accessed and shared. Analytic tools promote problem-solving and decision-making.
3. Business processes are well defined and documented to show employees the downstream impact of their activities and decisions.

Knowledge Acquisition

Define the source of knowledge and determine how it is acquired.

This is performed at Level 2: Tactical.

Description

Knowledge acquisition activities determines the source of knowledge and decides the most appropriate way in which it is acquired for use within the organization.

Knowledge acquisition involves complex process of reasoning, perception, and intuition. It takes thought, communication, association and reasoning to compile meaningful information in a way to be useful. Within an organization, knowledge should result in some sort of value. There is an inherent problem that exists with captured information; it does not stay current for long. On average, information within an U.S. based organization will change at a rate of two percent per month. This means that information will completely change, or become obsolete every three years. So those things that we once knew were true three years ago have changed. Employees make decisions based upon information that they believe is accurate and complete. When outdated information results in an inaccurate decision, the business will suffer and ultimately the customer will become dissatisfied.

The knowledge acquisition activities are tied to the strategic goals of the organization. The greater the ability to obtain quality information, the greater the odds will be to achieve the goals. Knowledge can be obtained both internally and from an external network or sources that can be used to support the strategic level decisions. Internal knowledge is used to improve quality and performance, and external knowledge is critical to respond to the customers to remain competitive. There are five primary external groups to source information: customers, suppliers, business partners and alliances, competitors, and industry communities.

External analysis is an essential component of the organizational strategy. However, many organizations do not have a defined strategy and approach to acquire and analyze information gained from these external groups. They rely on informal impressions, and intuition gained through tidbits of information received. As a result, the organization may make false assumptions and create blind spots where opportunities can be leveraged to improve a competitive advantage.

Gathering information to achieve a competitive advantage is not condoning corporate espionage or other illegal methods, rather it is a structured process to collect publically available information such as advertisements, news articles, product descriptions, corporate filings, and other sources used to help define market segments, product offerings, and other information that can be used to create a profile.

Desired Outcomes
A well-defined and structured plan is developed to acquire external information to create knowledge about the customer, competitors, and industry trends.

Inputs
The development of a knowledge management framework.

Tools and Techniques
- Interviews and focus groups
- Observation
- Knowledge modeling
- Kano Model
- Matrix decision grids
- Event diagrams and process maps
- Event maps

Metrics
Knowledge decay rate: The rate at which the information becomes less reliable.

Planning Considerations

The organization should profile the external groups: customers; suppliers; business partners and alliances; competitors; and industry communities. Knowledge comes in different forms that will need to be explored. This is knowledge for, about, and from the customers, and suppliers.

Collecting information about competitors is straight forward. It involves collecting, organizing and presenting the data, information, and knowledge that the firm has acquired in such a way that one can search, retrieve, and analyze it. Data mining and analysis using powerful IT systems are a valuable asset for this function.

Business partners, alliance partners must be closely managed. The key to gaining knowledge from these partners is the ability to foster trust. These partners have knowledge about products, markets, and suppliers. They have knowledge of specific distribution channels, products, and services that can be leveraged by the organization.

It is important to remember that the goal here is to create and foster two way learning; that a relationship will not last forever; and that a partner today may be a competitor tomorrow. KM must therefore be very aware of what knowledge is being shared, and the IT systems must reflect this policy.

Validation of Outcomes
1. Data sources have been identified for customers, suppliers, partners and competitors.
2. Data mining and analysis tools are used.

Knowledge Deployment

Develop an approach to share knowledge throughout the organization.

This is performed at Level 2: Tactical.

Description

In order to stabilize the change process, knowledge management is becoming more and more important. One of the most valuable resources for organizations is the tacit knowledge it gathers because it is essential to generate business best practices, competitive advantages, innovation, the ability to solve complex problems, and contribute to achieving maximum value in knowledge assets.

With a well-defined understanding of the vision and operational objectives, business units, department and work groups should have a strong understanding of their mission to effectively support the organization. However, each of these defined groups faces their own unique challenges to accomplish their mission. Each group has developed their own culture, a set of behaviors, knowledge, and beliefs that define how their work is accomplished. If provided with the right knowledge to solve their distinct issues or to leverage opportunities, their work group would not only benefit, it would collectively enhance the performance of the organization.

To create the tacit knowledge among the members of their particular work group, a structured knowledge deployment approach is used to generate business best practices and the ability to be innovative. There are four components that are iterative in developing and deploying specific knowledge within the organization:

- Experimenting: The group's action to prove their suppositions in order to discover something new to evaluate the impact.

- <u>Crossing boundaries</u>: The individuals give or receive information through the interaction with other individuals outside of the group.
- <u>Framing/reframing</u>: The individual's perception being transformed regarding an issue, situation or person in a new sense or significance.
- <u>Integrating perspectives</u>: The group members synthesize their diverging points of view and their apparent conflicts are resolved through dialog.

Specific collaborative activities are performed within each component to aid in the identification, definition, clarification, and validation of the information. Essential to the success of knowledge deployment is the ability for the members of these groups to work with autonomy to discover new ways through trial and error and to share their thoughts with others in an open and trusting environment. What is needed is to create a structure to incubate ideas and techniques, sharing them with others, transforming perceptions through reframing ideas and beliefs, and synthesizing differing viewpoints to continually improve to allow the organization to remain competitive.

Desired Outcomes
A knowledge approach and structure is created to foster the growth and development of new ideas in a safe and supportive work environment.

Inputs
- The creation of a knowledge management framework
- A knowledge acquisition approach
- Technical systems such as knowledge management systems and content management systems
- Defined and documented business processes
- Performance metrics
- A constructive and adaptive organizational culture

Tools and Techniques

- A problem-solving process and tool set
- SWOT analysis
- Data Analytic tools
- Knowledge maps
- Gap analysis/gap closure

Metrics

Operational process improvement: The percentage of increase in operational performance based upon changes made over a defined period of time.

Innovation conversion rate: The percentage of ideas and concepts that have been converted into practical solutions.

Planning Considerations

Creating a learning environment to develop knowledge among members of the organization starts with a clear vision and being able to clearly articulate that vision into every task that is performed. Hiring people who have the same values and beliefs is preferred over those who may have a skill. Create the physical environment that is conducive to innovation, exchanging thoughts, and working in groups. Then provide visible leadership not only to articulate the vision, but to remove obstacles for employees allowing them to be innovative, to experiment, and share their ideas.

Well-documented processes should be developed not as a control mechanism to limit what could be done but rather to achieve a common understanding among employees of customer and supplier requirements. A detailed process map will identify specific tasks that need to be accomplished by specific roles, and the technologies that will support the accomplishment of the task. Employees will have a better understanding of the consequences of their actions downstream.

The adoption of technology to enhance the process should focus on eliminating or reducing non-value added tasks and providing information at the right time, in the right format to aid the employee in making informed decisions. Access to complete information is critical to knowledge development.

Developing organizational knowledge requires cataloging its existing intellectual resources by creating a knowledge map. Knowledge can be characterized in many ways. Determine which method works best for your particular organization.

Create categories of knowledge by distinguishing between tacit and explicit knowledge, general and situated context-specific knowledge, and individual and collective knowledge. Knowledge can also be categorized by type, including declarative (knowledge about), procedural (know-how), causal (know-why), conditional (know when), and relational (know-with).

Map the organization's competitive knowledge position by performing a gap analysis. The gap between what a organization must do to compete and what it actually is doing represents a strategic gap. Addressing this gap provides the tactical areas that need to be addressed. Perform a SWOT analysis to identify the strengths and weaknesses that represent what the organization can do and the opportunities and threats that will dictate what it must do.

Validation of Outcomes
1. A culture and physical environment is created conducive to knowledge development.
2. The creation of a knowledge map that identifies the types and categories of knowledge and the resources that affect each area.
3. The ability to convert ideas into practical solutions to meet the evolving needs of their customers.

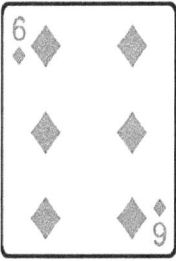

Reporting and Analytics

Identify metrics and predictive models by develop tools and techniques to measure performance.

This is performed at Level 3: Operational.

Description

Organizations are awash in data. Enterprise applications and other technical systems compile data from multiple sources and distribute it throughout the enterprise. This data is meaningless to employees unless it is placed in context and provides value; otherwise, it is just noise which can increase the level of complexity when making decisions.

Data, when put into a meaningful context, can become information which is needed when solving problems or making day-to-day decisions. However, too much information can become a distraction. Take, for example, the decision to dress for work. The data that we need is the current temperature, whether it is going to be cloudy, rain or snow, and whether it is going to be windy or not. With that information, you could dress appropriately. However, other climatic data such as barometric pressure, wind direction aloft, and annual rainfall are not important for the decision of getting dressed.

Obtaining the right information, at the right time, in the right format are critical factors in how information is interpreted to make decisions. Organizations often generate a wide assortment of reports. Reports often have defined parameters and reflect what occurred in the past. The information collected and displayed on a report provides a snapshot in time. This historical information can be used to forecast future trends or conditions. A report also is limiting in that it provides one dimension or viewpoint to what has occurred. Analytic tools aid in problem-solving and decision-making by providing multiple viewpoints and variables to provide the user with a holistic analysis.

Effective reporting and analytics solutions across the organization are critical for any organization trying to improve customer experience, drive sales transformation or reduce operational costs. All operating businesses need reporting and analytics to run. They need to analyze their problem areas to prioritize them for improvement. They need to report on the critical metrics of their business for compliance and control. And they need to communicate performance vs. targets throughout the organization and for each role.

As information systems mature and the aptitude of employees for working with data grow, reporting and analytics are becoming more pervasive inside companies. It has become standard for managers to know the relevant statistics on their business units, their core processes and the performance of their people. Personalized delivery of information is on its way to being universally accepted, even expected.

Desired Outcomes
Provide users with the right information, at the right time, in the right format, enabling them to make informed decisions that support the goals of the organization.

Inputs
- Knowledge of process activities and tasks for particular roles
- Governance rules on data access per role
- Decision-making criteria: timing, accuracy, quality, impact, etc.
- Content and knowledge management applications
- Technology tools used to generate and analyze data
- Quality of the data used to make decisions

Tools and Techniques
- Interviews and focus groups
- Knowledge mapping
- Determine purpose and outcomes from the report
- Analytic tools with access to data

Metrics

Quality decision ratio: The amount of value derived from decisions that are made based upon current and complete information.

Planning Considerations

Reports are created and used to account, validate or replicate data. Account reports are those that provide a statement of a situation as in budget reports, executive summaries or compliance reporting. These account reports are used to represent the business at a moment in time and represent a standard set of data. Validation reports are used to check a controlled process, such as quality checks, call volume or staffing levels. Reporting can be standard formats and times, or ad hoc. Replication data reports is a type of validation report that is used to compare data between systems. Reports have a defined purpose and are designed for a particular group of users to take specific actions. Reports are created using specific data points displayed for a given period of time. This information reflects actions that took place in the past and may not be an indicator of the future. Likewise, the data points selected and the period of time will provide a single viewpoint of the situation. For example, a report shows the amount of overtime worked was 120 hours over a period of a month, which may have exceeded the budget. This may be viewed negatively. However, the report did not show that orders for product surged by thirty percent over estimated volume, generating a healthy profit. Dashboards can replace traditional reports by providing, at a glance, a view of key performance indicators. The use of analytic or business intelligence tools enhances the ability to evaluate large quantities of data and scenarios to expedite potential solutions to allow employees to make informed choices.

Validation of Outcomes

Reports and analytic tools are used appropriately to make critical decisions.

Collaboration

Create a work environment to achieve a common business goal, and encourage open communication and collaborative problem-solving.

This is performed at Level 3: Operational.

Description

Collaboration is the ability to work together and share information to achieve a common goal. Collaboration is more than just communicating; it is the ability to interact with other people who share the same interests and beliefs to build and to work in partnership to develop ideas. Therefore, in order to generate this synergy, a collaborative environment needs to be created. The goal of collaboration is to bring together people to produce synergy around specific topics, in a specific location, with all related documents, tools and support material needed to achieve their stated goal.

There are a variety of collaboration tools currently available with many more being developed every day. However, we can group these tools into two types of collaboration:

- Asynchronous collaboration refers to methods and tools that relate to sharing information in one direction and does not require an immediate response. Examples of these tools include file sharing and workgroup team collaboration workspaces, as offered in content management systems. Website wikis are used for larger audiences where content is delivered via the Web and developed collaboratively by a community of users, allowing any user to add and edit content.
- Synchronous collaboration refers to methods and tools that facilitate two-way collaboration between two or larger numbers of people. Examples of these tools include instant messaging (IM), texting, screen sharing, VoIP audio conferencing, web conferencing, co-browsing, large audience webinars and virtual 3D immersive collaboration.

Most collaboration requires leadership, although the form of leadership can be social within a decentralized and unrestricted group. In particular, teams that work collaboratively can obtain greater resources, recognition and reward when facing competition for finite resources. Time must be allotted to allow members of teams to think and develop ideas, then to share those ideas with others.

Desired Outcomes
Create a collaborative environment by providing the tools, access to information, and the leadership to develop teams and partnerships with the same interests and goals.

Inputs
- Access to documents on a content management system and knowledge management system.
- Analytics and reporting tools available to the users.
- Operational processes that are defined by role.
- Well-defined goals with metrics and measures.

Tools and Techniques
- Mind mapping and diagramming
- Whiteboarding
- Scheduled collaboration sessions
- Consensus building techniques

Metrics
The quality of business solutions over a given period of time: Provides ideas and potential solutions generated through the collaborative process to solve business problems in a timely manner.

Planning Considerations
Collaboration is best performed in small groups to achieve the best desired result. The ideal group size is between four to seven people. Organizational leaders may make the assumption that large collaborative groups are desired to exchange ideas and share information across the

masses. The result is often general consensus rather than the ability to generate meaningful ideas.

Form groups based upon the interest of the members. Diverse backgrounds of the members generate unique ideas. A broad range of disciplines can provide varying points of view that may not have been considered by others.

There is much to be said about team dynamics. Individual personalities will range from boisterous to quiet or timid. A person with a zealous personality may bring enthusiasm and fun into the group. Whereas a quiet individual may listen, collect and process information before they provide input or make a decision. These personality types can be quite valuable, but, like anything, taken to the extreme it becomes a detriment to the group.

The collaboration team should try not to be hierarchical. When there is a dominant member with perceived or legitimate power, other members of the team may be intimidated and not contribute. When possible, try to select individuals who are at the same level within the organization.

Validation of Outcomes
1. Multiple small special interest groups are formed.
2. Employees are members of multiple groups.

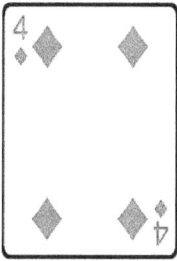

Organization and Team Learning

Create an iterative process that promotes risk taking, sharing information and constructive feedback.

This is performed at Level 3: Operational.

Description

To survive and grow in the current business environment, organizations are increasingly required to be sources of learning. Success, even survival, may be dependent on the extent to which the organization is able to learn, adapt and change. Rapid changes in the business environment necessitate organizations to create training and development programs to enhance their employees' adaptive abilities. Technological advances require the development of new skills. Corporate restructuring places greater responsibility on fewer workers and decision-making is pushed to lower levels — often self-managed teams. Cross-functional teams may be necessary for problem-solving across functional boundaries. Empowered employees who are accomplished problem solvers are needed to make informed decisions.

With all of the changes that occur within the organization, the question is: How does an organization learn? Organizational learning is a change in the knowledge that is embodied within an organization. "Learning" implies either a change that would directly improve the performance through skill development, or greatly alter the perception of what one thinks. In part, it is the experience of going through the change and realizing the effect of that change within the organization. As the organization matures, knowledge is maintained within small groups. New learning is formally documented and passed by word of mouth. Wisdom is then gained from the lessons learned from past experiences.

Knowledge in an organization can be embodied in devices, materials, facilities and infrastructure, people, and institutional knowledge within the organization. Such knowledge may be technological, but it may also

179

be other kinds related to the organization's operation, such as knowledge of the market in which it sells its products, or the markets from which it obtains goods and services, or knowledge of government regulations, or the general evolution of the economy, or many other topics.

Organizational learning as well as team learning has absolutely nothing to do with training. Learning in this context focuses on the transmission of both tacit and explicit knowledge throughout the group in addition to the creation of an environment in which focused creativity and knowledge sharing can flourish. Team learning and organizational learning is essentially the same; it is just performed on a different scale. The concepts of learning can be broken down into four key components: questioning, valuing diversity, communicating and learning review.

Desired Outcomes
Create a learning environment and process through the use of collaboration teams and tools.

Inputs
- Well-defined goals and clear operational objectives
- Access to information
- An organizational culture and work environment that support collaboration
- Defined operational business processes

Tools and Techniques
- The five why's technique
- Ishikawa diagrams — cause and effect
- Social networking applications
- Individual and group performance metrics and measures

Metrics
Competency gap: The gap between the desired level of operational performance and the current capabilities performed by the organization.

Planning Considerations

In order for an organization to develop a learning environment, the leadership must formulate a coherent vision of the future of the organization and how it would involve individual employees. This vision is supported by the core values, aligned to individual values. Learning is cultivated when the individual is empowered to explore new methods and the capacity to make choices to achieve the desired results.

Individuals working in small special interest teams focus their attention on developing a common awareness and perception that influence others through interaction. By continually talking about their mental models, they create a concept of how the organization should position itself, its products and its services to succeed.

Individual teams use mental models to create practical prototypes to test their theory. In the process, teams learn to understand the interdependencies and changes that shape the consequences of their actions. A system-based approach to learning aids in understanding the complexity and constraints that are imposed by the processes, technologies, resources and governances that dictate the organization's capability. As these teams work together, they not only create knowledge of their scope of expertise, but create an environment for organizational learning by the use of knowledge sharing using collaboration.

Validation of Outcomes

1. Organizational and team learning actions are performed through collaborative work groups.
2. The organization applies lessons learned to make changes in their systems and processes.
3. Knowledge from the teams is captured and shared across the organization.

Individual Learning and Development

Fulfill the gaps between current individual competencies and the requirements of the role, then develop a plan to foster growth and development.

This is performed at Level 4: Functional.

Description

The primary objective of the individual learning and development activity is to ensure all employees affected by the organizational change are identified and provided with the training needed to enable both individual and organizational capabilities. There are five critical success factors that need to be addressed: training environment, timing, performance, technical and functional availability, and resourcing. In order to learn new skills, an environment must be established where the student can focus on learning, can interact with other students and instructors, and can access the tools. Timing for learning is critical. New skills need to be developed and reinforced through trial and error. Ideally, just-in-time training provides a smooth transition between the training scenarios to the actual production environment. Providing training too early will allow the student to forget the skills learned. Performance standards need to be identified prior to training and aligned to the actual performance standards in production. Students should be provided with frequent feedback as they progress through training. The technical and functional systems in the training environment should mirror those in production. Differences can cause confusion, which will result in errors. Resourcing focuses on selecting the right employees to support the training activity. Instructors should be proficient in the skills taught and have an understanding of the overall process in which the skills are performed. Instructors must possess traits that can guide students with encouragement and support from beginning to end. In addition, instruction is a skill that needs to be perfected.

A Training strategy and framework provides a proven approach for successful transfer of knowledge and skills. The recommended training development is based upon the "ADDIE" model. This industry standard is a systematic instructional design model that consists of five phases: 1) Analysis, 2) Design, 3) Development, 4) Implementation, and 5) Evaluation. This framework works well with adult learning methods. During the implementation phase, the Tell-Show-Do-Review approach is preferred. This approach is proven to be the most effective way to deliver training to adult learners that is sustainable. The recommended evaluation method for the training utilizes the Kirkpatrick evaluation model to evaluate the effectiveness of the training preparation, execution and the overall sustainability. This model can be used with other learning processes, such as individual development, informal training and performance reviews. The Kirkpatrick evaluation model is a best practice that ensures an established delivery approach is provided at the right level, to offer value to the organization. This evaluation model has been adopted extensively throughout the industry.

Desired Outcomes
The gaps in skills between the current state and the desired state are identified using a structured approach and delivered using adult education methods, along with a variety of training techniques. Evaluation measures are used to ensure that the appropriate delivery approach is used, at the right level, at the right time, to provide value to the individual.

Inputs
- Well-defined organizational and team learning approach and plan.
- Technical systems (applications and databases) that can be used for training and user experimentation.
- Current and future-state operational business processes defined by roles.
- Job role competencies.

Metrics
Operational performance over time: The sustained level of performance during and after the change initiative.

Tools and Techniques
- ADDIE model for instructional systems design
- Kirkpatrick evaluation model

Planning Considerations

Using the Tell-Show-Do-Review method is a proven learning approach that provides grounding in adult learning principles and allows for support of differences in learning styles. The approach elements for developing training material are:
- Tell: The learner is provided with relevant information about the task, and why it is important. Hearing this information explained will satisfy the needs of the auditory learner.
- Show: The learner will observe a demonstration of the task to discover how it is performed correctly. The visual stimulus will satisfy the needs of the visual learner.
- Do: The learner will perform the task and demonstrate the ability to perform it correctly. This tactile act satisfies the needs of the tangible learner.
- Review: After performing the task, the learner will be corrected for any errors, and provided with feedback, encouragement, and additional information to ensure understanding of the task. This form of feedback reinforces the learning to produce longer lasting results.

Understanding the principles of adult learning will enhance the learning experience and create an environment for continuous learning throughout the organization. Listed below are guidelines for adult learning.

Create a Supportive Environment: Convey respect for individuals and the belief and value in the learning process. Draw on previous experiences of participants.

Use Training Methods that Require Active Participation: Active participation engages trainees in the learning process and enhances retention of new concepts.

Use a Variety of Teaching Methods: Not all people learn the same way. Individual learning styles are influenced by personality, intelligence, education, experience, culture, and sensory and cognitive preferences.

Provide Structured Learning Opportunities: Empower trainees to be self-directed learners as they strive to fulfill objectives of the training, by teaching them how to master the content and become aware of their own learning process.

Provide Immediate Feedback on Practice: Providing timely corrective feedback leads to successful learning and mastery of content and skills. Sensitive feedback helps trainees' correct errors and reinforces desired behaviors.

Meet Trainee's Individual Learning Needs: Effective trainers never forget they have a group of individual learners with varying abilities, experiences and motivations.

Make Course Content Relevant and Coherent: Begin with the basics and build on each part in sequential order when presenting course content.

Validation of Outcomes
1. Employees (stakeholders) identified who are directly impacted by change.
2. Skill gaps have been identified and gap closure plan developed.
3. A variety of training materials and delivery methods used based upon adult learning principles.
4. Evaluation models are put in place to measure gap closure.

Internalization

Implement a process to align organizational beliefs, attitudes and values with individuals within the organization.

This is performed at Level 4: Functional.

Description

Change, whether perceived as good or bad, can be promoted rather easily in an organization through a domino effect. Internalization is a process by which the change is communicated through various channels over time among people within the organization. Each person within an organization undergoing change faces his/her own decision to accept and embrace the change, or reject it, will progress through five phases listed below.

1. Knowledge — person becomes aware of the change and has some idea of how it functions.
2. Persuasion — person forms a favorable or unfavorable attitude toward the change initiative.
3. Decision — person engages in activities that lead to a choice to adopt or reject the change.
4. Implementation — person puts the change activities into use.
5. Confirmation — person evaluates the results of the change decision already made.

The most striking feature of internalization is that, for most members of an organization, the decision to change depends heavily on the decisions of the other members of the organization. Research shows that after about ten to twenty-five percent of the members adopt the change, there is a relatively rapid adoption by the remaining members and then a period in which the holdouts finally adopt.

The decision to adopt change is made through a cost/benefit analysis where the major obstacle is uncertainty. People will adopt if they believe that it will, all things considered, enhance overall value. So, they must believe that the proposed change may yield some relative advantage to the idea it supersedes. How can they know for sure that there are benefits? Also, in consideration of costs, people determine to what degree the changes would disrupt other facets of their daily life. *Is it compatible with existing habits and values? Is it hard to use? It sounds good, but does it work? If I adopt it, will other people think I'm weird?*

To accelerate adoption of change, the structured eight-step process developed by Dr. John P. Kotter is recommended to improve the ability to change. Organizations can increase their chances of success, both today and in the future. Without this ability to adapt continuously, organizations cannot thrive. These steps include: develop a sense of urgency; build a guiding coalition for the change; create a clear vision; communicate the vision, empower people to make change; create short term wins; never let up; and incorporate the change in future activities.

Desired Outcome
Individuals working within groups will perceive value and adopt quickly to the change.

Inputs
- Collaborative teams in place to exchange information and share ideas or concerns
- Information about the issues and opportunities that drive the change
- Defined roles and responsibilities with the change initiative

Metrics
The amount of early adopters and early majority over a defined time period: Ability to measure the amount of employees who accept the change early in the initiative.

Tools and Techniques

- Communication strategy and plan
- Focus groups, workshops
- Surveys and polls
- Team building activities
- Identify and support change agents
- Short-term wins
- Goal setting
- Process improvement

Planning Considerations

Leaders need to create a sense of urgency that will gain the attention of the individual employee, compelling enough to make him/her take action. Leaders often underestimate how difficult it is to drive people out of their comfort zones, or make assumptions that the individual employee already understands the level of importance. Employees should realize that the change is effectively managed, and that there is no need to panic and make rash decisions because the level of urgency has increased. The change vision should describe how it will personally affect the individual and the value it will have on the organization.

Every employee should be involved in the change process, not just the designated project team. Those people not chosen to participate on the project need to take on additional work, allowing the project team members to focus on the change initiative. In addition, they need to be recognized for their contributions. During the transition, process improvements and extra customer care need to be addressed since normal business operations are often disrupted.

Change management guru John P. Kotter, a professor at Harvard Business School and world-renowned change expert, introduced his eight-step change process in his 1995 book, *Leading Change*. Kotter's eight steps for leading change are described below:

1. **Establishing a Sense of Urgency** — Identify and communicate the need to change.
2. **Creating the Guiding Coalition** — Assemble and empower a change team.
3. **Developing a Change Vision** — Create a clearly defined vision for change.
4. **Communicating the Vision for Buy-in** — Use multiple vehicles to communicate the vision.
5. **Empowering Broad-based Action** — Develop a plan to identify and remove barriers to achieve the vision.
6. **Generating Short-term Wins** — Perform performance improvements during the initiative and recognize and reward those employees who were involved.
7. **Never Letting Up** — Create an environment of continuous change that supports and aligns to the vision.
8. **Incorporating Changes into the Culture** — Align the leadership, management styles, systems and structures to the core values to create an adaptive and constructive culture.

Validation of Outcomes
1. Employees understand the issues and opportunities; they know the sense of urgency and can describe the vision for change.
2. Employees are empowered to take action, be involved in the change process, and are encouraged to participate in the change process.
3. Ideas and recommendations are encouraged and acted upon.
4. New behaviors are recognized and rewarded.

Problem-Solving and Decision-Making

Create processes, tools and techniques that will improve decision-making and the quality of decisions.

This is performed at Level 4: Functional.

Description

Employees solve problems and make decisions every day. Managers rely on their employees to identify issues, understand the requirements and their associated controls, and to make decisions that are beneficial to their customers and to the business. Individual problem-solving may not be viewed as an issue in daily business operations since the solution is difficult to qualify in terms of results such as market share, customer satisfaction, quality, performance or other measures of outcome.

The ability to perform effective problem-solving and make informed decisions stems from the integration of the four drivers of performance: a highly qualified and motivated workforce; efficient business processes; technical capabilities that will automate workflow and provide tools that will aid in the display and analysis of the data; and the ability of the employee to access current and complete information. The ability to get the right information, at the right time, in the right format to make an informed decision is a critical element of the decision process. Having a knowledge worker who is highly motivated and supported by a constructive and adaptive organizational culture that embraces collaboration provides the other critical element.

Many employees can struggle to create a viable solution that offers a high degree of value, and an outcome that is accepted and supported by customers and the organization, when they do not have the right information, the right tools and the right support. A great solution is worthless if the team did not actively participate in the process to create buy-in and support. Likewise, if the team quickly comes to an agreement without properly analyzing the problem or the solution alternatives, then the resulting decision will be of poor quality. The team must work together in an intersection of common goals. This act of people working together constructively to achieve a common purpose is called collaboration. Collaborative problem-solving is part art and part science. To achieve a high-quality solution acceptable to the group members requires a collaborative effort, a structured process with well-defined tools, and the knowledge and skill to use them effectively. Problem-solving is much more effective when performed in a collaborative group. A study has found that groups of three to five people perform better than individuals when solving complex problems. The study, published in the April 2008 issue of the *Journal of Personality and Social Psychology*, suggests that groups of three people are able to solve difficult problems better than even the best individuals working alone. "The whole is greater than the sum" in high-performing teams.

Desired Outcomes
Highly skilled and motivated individuals working in a collaborative team environment can effectively problem-solve and make quality decisions when provided with complete and accurate data, and analytic tools to aid in the process.

Inputs
- Access to complete and accurate information
- Technical tools such as reporting and analytics
- Defined operational business processes indicating roles
- A constructive and adaptive organizational culture that supports collaboration

Metrics
The metrics on the quality of problem-solving and decision-making are defined in the respective tasks that this function supports.

Tools and Techniques
- A collaborative problem-solving process
- Reporting and analytic tools (software applications)

Planning Considerations

A structured problem-solving process should be used to provide employees with a common approach and set of tools that can be used throughout the organization. The structured approach provides consistency, reducing the need to retrain employees.

Effective problem-solving requires two primary components: a quality solution and the acceptance of the solution. There are four parts that will support the process: rational skills that provide the ability to think clearly and sensibly; individual competencies; interpersonal skills and processes such as listening, supporting and participating; and behavioral styles that are influenced by the operational culture.

Problems come to light when the activities are measured against the defined metrics and key performance indicators. The problems should describe the situation that you want to influence as it currently exists, and as objectively as possible.

Employees must be empowered to make decisions within the scope of their authority. Decisions must be based on providing value to the customer and the business. A logical and systematic decision-making process helps address the critical elements that result in a good decision.

Validation of Outcomes
1. A structured, collaborative problem-solving approach implemented
2. Sound decision-making processes are used with empowered employees
3. Employees are provided with the tools they need to facilitate problem-solving and decision-making
4. Complete and accurate information is provided at the right time, and the right format
5. Employees have the competencies and are empowered to make decisions within their scope of influence

Section Four:

Playing the Game

Defining Leadership

The remaining topic that will need to be addressed before moving forward is the leadership style that is required for a successful change. I had to evaluate the character traits needed for a major transformation of the business. A meeting was setup with Mr. Schein, the boss, to discuss the commitment requirements needed to ensure success.

Mr. Schein told me he was a former U.S. Marine Corps officer. He stated that although the new game provided a well-defined methodology and approach to complete the mission, he reaffirmed that a strong leader is needed to guide the initiative. I agreed with him, and we shared past experiences about his effectiveness as the strong, visible leader.

He had pulled out an article from the *Legacy* newsletter, which was written about Fred Smith, founder of the highly successful FedEx Corporation, who acknowledged that the Marine Corps played a vital role in shaping his life. He also noted the business achievements of other marines in the corporate world. Smith was quoted in the article saying, "Nothing has prepared business leaders better for their roles in business and society than the lessons they learned in the Corps — lessons of discipline, organization, commitment and integrity." Everything about the Marines — their culture, their organizational structure, their management style and their decision-making process — is geared toward creating a high-speed, high-complexity environment. This situation is similar to those elements found in large-scale change initiatives within organizations.

There are three fundamental categories that every U.S. Marine is instructed in: leadership objectives, leadership traits and leadership principles. Business leaders would benefit from learning and applying these lessons in their organization.

There are two leadership objectives. The primary objective of Marine Corps leadership is mission accomplishment. This requires a goal-oriented approach. A leader must identify long-term goals for the team and the short-term steps the organization needs to take to achieve those goals. The secondary objective of leadership is troop (employee) welfare —also described as team welfare or individual welfare. This objective requires empathy on the part of the leader to make sure that the needs of those in the team are looked after.

There are fourteen traits to which all marines are encouraged to aspire. They are judgment, justice, dependability, integrity, decisiveness, tact, initiative, enthusiasm, bearing, unselfishness, courage, knowledge, loyalty and endurance. Marines are encouraged to exhibit these traits and are judged on their ability to do so. The official Marine Corps website defines the leadership traits in greater detail. When these leadership traits are applied within business, they aid in the development of a strong, adaptive and constructive culture that encourages all employees to do their best.

Marines are encouraged to memorize and are often required to recite the fourteen leadership traits at inspections, but it is not required for them to memorize the definitions. The Marine Corps would rather its marines contemplate what they mean for themselves. One might assume the Marine Corps does this to ensure individuals internalize these traits by coming up with their own definitions. The same is true about attaching priorities to these traits. For instance, is judgment a more important trait than decisiveness? The Marine Corps leadership system doesn't specify, unlike the leadership objectives which are described in terms of "primary" and "secondary."

The last component of the Marine Corps leadership system is the set of Marine Corps leadership principles. Like the objectives and traits, these principles are given to marines to set goals for their attitudes and behaviors. I will state these leadership principles in business terms:

Know yourself and seek self-improvement. No matter how much leaders achieve, there is always room for improvement. One can never have too much knowledge or too many skills. Business leaders should try to live a lifestyle of continual growth.

Develop a sense of responsibility among your employees. No one can be everywhere all the time. By developing responsibility among employees throughout the entire organization, an individual doesn't have to be. The business leaders should empower their employees to make decisions and hold them accountable.

Be technically and tactically proficient. All employees should be trained thoroughly in the mechanics of their job and rigorously tested at least annually in basic skills of their profession. This includes their ability to problem-solve and make informed decisions.

Make sound and timely decisions. To be effective, business leaders should couple decisiveness with judgment. Know your employees and look out for their welfare. The Marine Corps understands that people are its most valuable resource and so should business leaders. By knowing whom best to delegate tasks to, leaders are then able to accomplish their missions efficiently.

Keep Your Employees Informed. "Ours is not to reason why, ours is but to do and die." This popular maxim repeated in a scene in *Saving Private Ryan* perpetuates the idea that marines blindly follow orders. While it is true that time does not allow for an explanation in all instances, when time is available, marines are told the "why" behind the orders. Business leaders must ensure that their employees understand the goals of the organization as well as how they fit into the overall scheme. Leaders need to talk to their employees often, even if it's just to say that everything is going according to plan.

Seek responsibility and take responsibility for your actions. By taking on responsibility, leaders show that they have confidence in their own abilities. Likewise, when leaders make mistakes, they are encouraged to own up to it. Admitting to their mistakes shows integrity and maturity.

Ensure assigned tasks are understood, supervised and accomplished. Leaders should be very specific about exactly want they want done and who will be responsible for its completion. Strong leaders set deadlines or benchmarks, and they follow up. By being very specific about what needs to be accomplished, the "how" of the task should get pushed as far down the chain of command as possible. This allows for a great deal of flexibility at the smallest group level.

Train your employees as a team. If an organization has the best employees in the world, it will be meaningless if they don't work together in a coordinated fashion. Make sure that the lines of communication are open among departments. Time should be spent cross training work groups so that each unit has an understanding of the other unit's responsibilities.

These objectives, principles and traits are built around simple truths about human nature and the uncertainties of dynamic work environments. Obviously, these are factors that can have a great impact on any organization. The difference is that the Marines have staked their life on them, which is a strong motivation to getting it right.

The success of transformational change is incumbent upon strong leadership principles and traits. Mr. Schein was able to use his leadership characteristics to develop and bring out the best in the men and women who will lead the tracks of work in each performance area.

Selecting the Change Champions

After the discussion that I had with Mr. Schein, I felt confident that leadership at the top was intact, and that he would be actively involved in the decision-making process as well as motivating and driving the change vision to fruition.

Now it was time to cascade the authority of the change initiative to the owners of each track of work. These owners are the change champions, those who possess the leadership traits and capabilities described on the card indicating the "King" of each suit.

The change champion offers a unique set of skills and personality traits. Above all, a change champion must be a recognized leader with legitimate power and authority. He/she must be respected among peers and subordinates. What makes change champions truly unique is that they are somewhat rebellious against the status quo. They are not satisfied with the way the organization currently operates, and will seek to gain new insights and explore new ways to add value. The information, along with a criteria rating form, can be found in Appendix B. A list of characteristics and personality traits are used in a criteria rating form as a guide to select the most appropriate person for the role.

Change champions will be the core of the operational planning team. They are temporarily reassigned to this special project with the responsibility to plan, guide and coordinate this initiative. This core team is the nucleolus of the leadership command that will guide the project team to complete the stated goal.

The mission that Mr. Schein wants for his organization is both broad and complex. Due to the scope and multifaceted elements inherent within a large-scale transformation initiative, the change champions will assume responsibility of his/her specific performance track of work to ensure the activities and tasks are not only completed, but desired outcomes are achieved.

In addition to leadership skills to guide the transformation, they will be involved with critical thinking, conceptual planning and visualization with the project team, using a structured approach and tools.

Critical thinking involves the high-order cognitive skills of analysis, synthesis and evaluation. Analysis allows the team to identify all of the elements, and then recognize patterns and interpret the results. Synthesis allows team members to make predictions, draw conclusions and create ideas. The team will be able to discuss "what-if" situations that develop new ideas. Evaluation allows planners to critique ideas, make recommendations, assess value and make choices. All three high-order thinking skills are required in the transformation process.

Conceptual planning allows the change champions to work with the team members to develop an understanding of the culture, as well as expansion of a broad approach to solve the problem. This type of planning allows creative ideas to be identified and evaluated using defined criteria.

Visualization is the leader's picture of how the organization will look in the future. This image provides team members with a mental image of how the organization will appear and how employees will operate in the coming years. The stronger this image, the greater the ability will be to create and execute plans to build this future state.

****

Using the criteria rating guide, Mr. Schein selected the change champions for the initiative. After meeting with his selected candidates, explaining their new responsibilities and commitment, they agreed to support the new initiative.

The first activity among this group of five leaders was for Mr. Schein to outline his goals and expectations. It is critically important for each member of this senior leadership team to understand the issues that the organization currently faces, and for everyone to agree to the goal and direction that is needed for success.

During these meetings, the leaders will focus on creating the change vision. This vision describes how the organization will look, feel and operate at a future point in time. This is the message that must be communicated to the project team and throughout the organization. This vision must guide the actions and decisions of the team to create systems and align the organization to accomplish this goal.

Along with the creation of the vision for change is defining the sense of urgency to change. The leadership team must be able to define the reason why the organization is taking this action and what difference the change will make.

The leadership team describes in realistic terms the pain points along with the consequences. There may be a number of issues that have created the current situation. The cause of these issues may not be clear at this point in time. There also may be a number of assumptions that need to be validated. Potential causes to these issues will be discovered as the project team moves through each activity of the integrated performance process.

At the end of the meeting, the leaders must have a single, clear message to communicate to the project team and throughout the organization. They must be able to communicate the vision for change and describe the sense of urgency to move forward. Mr. Schein and the four change champions are now prepared to meet with the rest of the players to start the game.

Getting the Stakeholders Together

All of the players were assembled in the back room prepared to start the new game. As we got situated, we heard comments of skepticism and doubt that this new game was not any different from what they already knew. The players had reviewed each card and said that they had a good understanding of the activities and tasks that were described. They stated that there was nothing new or unique about these activities and tasks, just that there were fifty-two of them. One of the players said some of the activities and tasks on the cards were irrelevant to perform each and every time a major change was introduced, while another player said that there were many more tasks that were not listed. These comments added to the distrust and uncertainty among the players.

It wasn't until the big boss, Mr. Schein, stood up and spoke directly to the group:

> "Each time we entered into a major project, the odds were that it was going to fail. Research proves this fact; it states that seventy percent of all large-scale change initiatives fail to meet budget, time and/or scope. Budgets exceed expectations by twenty-eight percent on average. They go over time by thirty percent, and the scope is generally reduced by one third."

In addition, Mr. Schein went on to say that past projects had failed to meet stated expectations because the focus was on implementing new software, or enhancing technical features or functionality rather than solving the business problem. Although the technical enhancements were nice to have and provided improvements, they did not provide the overall value needed by the business.

Mr. Schein was willing to try this new approach and expressed his strong desire that every one of the players show open support for the new game. He said that the first rule of this new game was to have one primary leader of the change initiative and that leader would be Mr. Schein himself. He would guide and direct the subordinate leaders to achieve the goal of creating the change based upon the change vision. Mr. Schein insisted on loyalty to ensure every player not only understands what was required of every person in the room, but also their commitment to the success of the project.

Failure not to play by these rules did not have to be explained further. Everyone knew by the commitment and directness from Mr. Schein that there would be consequences if they were not onboard. They all knew that the survival of the organization is at stake, and everyone must work together in order to win.

Mr. Schein introduced the four change champions to the stakeholders at the game. He described the roles they would play in this initiative. He said they act somewhat like a pit boss by leading and coordinating activities. They also work like a coach to motivate and encourage stakeholders to align to the vision, while assisting to solve problems as they arise.

He went on to describe the way in which the activities and tasks are grouped into the four suits led by the change champions who were represented by the king of their respective suit.

The King of Hearts will address all of the activities associated with the people and the organization, such as the design of jobs, reporting relationships, organizational culture, motivation and satisfaction.

The King of Clubs will address the business processes impacted by the change. The value chain, business requirements, activities and tasks, and performance levels are addressed in this track.

The King of Spades addresses the technical systems and functionality to enhance the business performance.

The King of Diamonds will address the way in which information is accessed and used throughout the organization. It also addresses how the organization learns and applies what it learns to improve.

Dealing the Cards

The players sat down at the large table somewhat hesitant amid all of the changes. The cards were dealt, all face up. "How can we play like that when everyone can see our hand?" exclaimed one of the players. "That is just the point," Mr. Schein stated. "We are not playing against each other; we are playing against our competitors, providing our customers with the products and services they want and desire, along with our ability to be flexible and rapidly change when required. With the cards face up, each one of us can see what everyone has in terms of information and resources. By thinking and working in a team, we can work collaboratively to plan and coordinate our actions."

All of the cards are dealt in front of the players. The cards represent very specific activities and tasks that are essential for each level within the performance track. The cards are distributed in front of all of the stakeholders to provide an understanding of what will be required to achieve the mission and to begin the process of tapping into the tribal knowledge among the various functional areas. These pockets of knowledge that exist within departments and other functional areas will be shared among the stakeholders, helping to understand the issues and aid in diagnosing the problem within the business. An important aspect of the game is not only to complete the activities and tasks within the track of work, but to work collaboratively between the other groups to determine the potential impact that a change in one area will have on other areas. This will be explained in greater detail later. For now, it is important for the players to understand the following:

- All of the players work together as a unified team to solve the stated problem and achieve the vision.
- The activities and tasks are defined and understood by all of the players.
- Although activities are assigned to specific groups, they will all work together to determine the potential impact that an activity will have on the other activities.

Sorting the Cards

As stated earlier, each suit represents a performance driver containing related activities and tasks. They are considered drivers of performance within the organization because each area provides a level of functionality or desired behavior that is judged by the leadership by its effectiveness and overall value. Each track of work is focused on driving performance within their scope and influence as defined by the initiative.

Each suit represents a functional area of thirteen related activities, defined by each card which will need to be accomplished at a specific time. An activity is comprised of two or more tasks. A task is a single unit of work comprised of work steps which are often referred to as procedures.

Each activity is placed in a hierarchical structure to provide order in which it should be performed. The hierarchy that is used corresponds to the way that business is planned and executed. There are four levels of hierarchy: strategy, tactical, operational and functional level.

The strategic level provides a plan of action needed to accomplish a mission or high-level goal. A strategic plan would determine not only to achieve a defined target, but to create a vision of how things may be after the target has been accomplished. A strategic mission plan in the military is not just winning the war, but restoring the country to a peaceful lifestyle. In business, strategic plans may not just be defined to meet sales goals, but to achieve customer loyalty with all of the products and services the business provides. A strategic change initiative may look at a component of the organization and transform its business operation into something new and different. However, the strategy must also be concerned with the integration of the change into the existing business operation without major disruption. In order for the strategy to be successful, it must be divided into tactical components.

The tactical level provides more specificity from one or more areas to align and support the strategic plan. In a business, the tactical areas can be thought of as specific departments, such as finance, human resources, supply chain, sales, marketing, and so forth. They can also be defined as testing, communication, project management and other project-related groups. Each one of these units provides products and services that support and align to the overall business strategy. They are incapable of operating by themselves and rely on the other units to provide value. Tactical activities are still at a high level because they focus on the combined capabilities of the specific work track to support the business strategy. The tactical activities in the change initiative are aligned to the change strategy by focusing on meeting the specific requirements in the project.

The operational level provides the detail components to support and sustain a particular operation. These activities and tasks are unique to that particular unit, system or function. As an example, a particular business unit may have a flat organizational structure, staffed with employees who have a precise skill set. The business unit may require a specific software application and generate reports to evaluate and control their operation. Within the context of the change initiative, the activities focus on examining various elements within the units that are within the scope of the change initiative, including the systems, processes and functions.

The functional level provides a focus on individual tasks that are part of the activities impacted by the change. This is the smallest level of detail, yet critical to ensure success. As an example, a software application may require defining a field on the screen, or a task may need to be broken down to individual work steps in order for an employee to perform it consistently.

In the new game, each card represents an activity that has a face value that corresponds to the one of the levels. Each suit represents one of the four performance drivers: People/Organization; Business Process; Technology; and Information/Knowledge Management.

Three cards of the same suit are aligned to each level within the performance driver. This reduces the level of complexity when managing the change initiative.

- The King of each suit is the change champion of that performance driver, as stated earlier. Although the change champion is a strategic activity, it is designed to influence every activity in the performance track.
- The Queen, Jack and 10 cards comprise activities at the strategic level.
- The 9, 8 and 7 cards comprise activities at the tactical level.
- The 6, 5 and 4 cards comprise activities at the operational level.
- The 3, 2 and Ace comprise tasks at the functional level.

Prime Activities

With the cards sorted out between the tracks of work and the performance levels, it creates a matrix of sixteen groups of activities. This matrix reduces the complexity of implementing the transformation. These groups of activities are designed to align the organization from its current state to bring the future state to fruition, one level at a time.

Selected groups of activities are designated as primary activities. These prime activities aid in driving and shaping the organization to realize the transformation. There is one set of prime activities per level used to drive and shape the change. The other groups of activities are no less important, but are designed to support and align with the prime activity at that particular level.

Start Here	People/ Organization	Business Process	Technology	Information/ Knowledge Management
Strategic Level 1				
Tactical Level 2			Finish Here	
Operational Level 3				
Functional Level 4				

Figure 2: Prime Activities

Designating prime groups of activities further reduces the complexity that is inherent within large change initiatives and allows the change champions, project team members and stakeholders to understand the changes from the strategic level, which tends to be more conceptual in nature, and will move down levels and across each performance driver to the detailed functional level.

To illustrate how the primary activities will aid in defining the transformation initiative, I will start at the strategic level, under the people and organization track of work. The prime activities include clarifying the core values of the organization; developing a vision to change; and defining the guiding principles. Clarifying the organization's core values helps to align project team members and stakeholders to the morals and operating principles which the organization founded. It essentially states what behaviors are acceptable to accomplish the transformation goals. Once understood, the vision for change is defined in terms of how the organization will operate in the future. It emphasizes the sense of urgency to change, along with clear goals the leadership expects to achieve. The guiding principles state the standards which the project team will follow to transition the current state of the organization to a new way of behaving and interacting with customers and suppliers. It also serves as a personal code of conduct that shows the way to work as a team. Now that the vision, goals and operating principles are defined, the project team has a conceptual understanding of what direction the organization wants to move, and what needs to change to accomplish the goals.

The next prime activity is at the tactical level under the business process track of work. The scope of the strategic change vision is defined in part by the business processes that are impacted. The prime activities include identifying high-level business requirements; identify critical business processes; and analyze the performance of these critical processes. In addition, the current level of performance is used as a baseline to measure the impact of the change. The future-state processes will be created and will incorporate best practices. This will be compared with the current state process where a gap analysis and gap closure plan will be created. Upon completion of the tactical tasks, the project team will have a clear understanding of the scope, the degree of change required, and a high-level understanding of what needs to change.

Once the tactical business requirements and processes have been identified, along with the current performance level, the next set of prime activities will focus on the operational tools needed to enhance the process.

These tools are used to enhance the business processes by integrating systems, reducing non-value related administrative tasks through automation, and speeding up the process by automated workflow. Other technologies that support the operational level may include the ability of the workforce to work mobile, access information remotely, and collaborate with employees, customers and suppliers. To ensure that the technology works according to plan, a support structure is then needed to maintain the infrastructure.

The last set of prime activities is found at the functional level, controlled by the information and knowledge management track. The sole purpose is to provide the individual employee with the information and competencies they need to effectively problem-solve and make informed decisions. When employees are provided with useful information, they learn to synthesize it, develop new innovative ideas, and learn from past mistakes. At this point, the change vision is internalized by each individual; the business requirements and processes are defined and measured; and the technical capabilities have enhanced the business processes as well as provided the tools to assist the individual to perform their job in the most efficient way possible. Then the individual employee, armed with the information and the tools, can be empowered to operate at a greater level of performance.

The prime activities described above help to provide a focus not only for the project team members, but also for the other employees throughout the organization. The entire organization needs to understand why the change is needed and support the selected members of the initiative. They need to know how the change will occur and what will actually change. In addition, everyone in the organization needs to see that the project is progressing successfully. The prime activities at each level aid in providing a specific focus. The leadership along with the organizational change management team can use the prime activities to communicate changes. The transition from the strategic, tactical, operational and functional levels provides key milestones that can be celebrated. The entire organization is taken along on the change journey as the transformation takes place. This makes it possible for a smooth transition toward realizing the future state.

Integrating the Activities

As previously stated, prime activities are the focal point the other activities align for that particular level. It is important to understand the relationships that exist between the set of activities across each level. These related tasks may be presented as barriers or enablers to change.

Starting from the strategic level, the prime activities define the change vision, values and guiding principles. Once defined, examination of the value chain, compliance requirements and business policies may create constraints that may limit the ability of the initiative to achieve the stated goals. Leveraging the technical architectural principles may dictate how the technology may be deployed, such as how cloud computing is utilized. This may define how information is stored and accessed. The organizational values may influence the social networking philosophy, such as if networking will be allowed, which social sites will be used, and how are they used to support the business. As the strategy planning progresses, specific activities may need to be defined, or changed to meet the new requirements of the change vision.

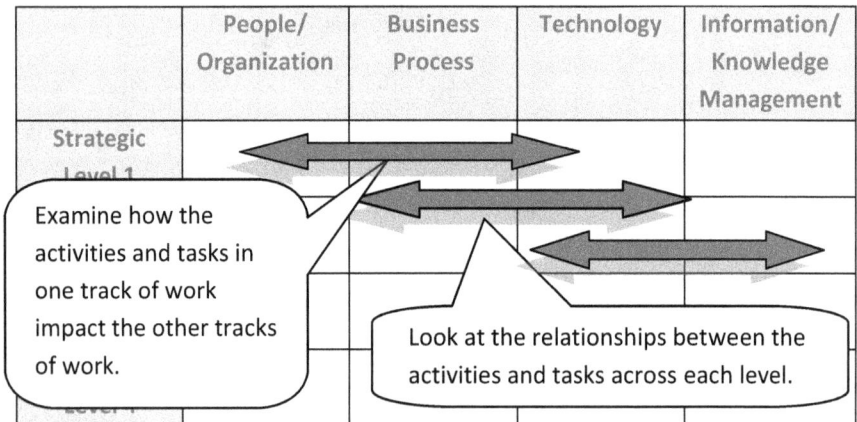

	People/ Organization	Business Process	Technology	Information/ Knowledge Management
Strategic Level 1				

Examine how the activities and tasks in one track of work impact the other tracks of work.

Look at the relationships between the activities and tasks across each level.

Figure 3: Integrated Activities

There is a cause-and-effect relationship that will take place between each set of activities. Changes in one area may have an impact on associated activities in that level. In addition, changes made to one or more activities will most likely have an impact on subordinate activities in the lower levels.

	People/ Organization	Business Process	Technology	Information/ Knowledge Management
Strategic Level 1				
Complete all of the activities and tasks at this level **first** before proceeding to the next level.				

Figure 4: Cascading Activities to the Next Level

Before the project team advances to the next level, they must insure that every set of activities has been completed and that the activities have been integrated across their current level. Validation that an activity is complete requires more than just checking a box. To successfully complete the activity it must achieve the desired outcome in measurable terms. Once an acceptable level has been achieved, then, and only then should the activity be considered complete. Since every change initiative is uniquely different, the activities in the matrix are defined broad enough to address most situations in a project, yet specific enough to provide value. Therefore, the project team must determine how each activity influences the other areas in terms of desired outcomes. When we examine the activities in the tactical level, for example, we first address the prime activities: high-level business requirements; documented critical business processes; and performance of the process. The outcomes of these activities will aid in defining the key performance indicators and the service-level agreements, and determining performance metrics aligned to the change vision from the people and organization track of work. The technical team would determine the ability for the network and infrastructure to support the changes in the business process. They will also evaluate the systems and applications currently in production if they can enhance the new process through integration and automation. The change in the business process will change the way in which knowledge is developed and deployed. Likewise, the technical systems need to enable the acquisition of knowledge. Working together, the project team will be able to integrate the outcomes from each activity to meet the performance and change requirements for each level as the project progresses.

* * *

The players now appear to be actively involved in the game. The back room has taken on an entirely different look and feel. The players have formed into functional teams focusing on their activities and sharing information with other team members to achieve their desired outcomes. Although change is serious business, the members show respect for the other members. Conversations are friendly and easy going — a major change from the old game. The change champions lead their groups through the change initiative by reinforcing the vision and removing barriers for the project team members to perform their tasks.

The path to achieving the goals, and ultimately the mission, is clearly defined and uncomplicated. The cards are face up on the table where everyone can see what activities need to be accomplished, including the desired outcomes required to support and align with the change vision. A new set of collaborative tools have been introduced to analyze problems, generate potential solutions and coordinate the implementation of the solutions. Select metrics are used to define what is important to measure along the change journey, and measurements are taken to determine if the project team remains on target. The vision for change will become crystal clear to all of the employees as the project team moves from the strategic level to the details of the functional level. Acceptance of change by the leadership, the project team, the stakeholders and the entire organization is accomplished when:

- there is a sense of urgency to change that is understood by all,
- the vision for change is both clear and meaningful,

- the path to transform the organization is clearly defined and straight forward,
- there are obvious milestones at frequent intervals,
- metrics and measures to assess the progress for change are meaningful,
- collaboration and active participation to drive toward meaningful change by everyone is not only expected, but part of the culture, and
- the goal is clearly defined and understood by all.

My work as the hired gun is now finished. It's time for me to mosey down the road to find a new card game and avoid being shot by the old timers who are set in their ways. I am confident that the new game will live on and will continue to be played as the organization continues to change.

Winning

Success and the ability for an organization to accomplish its defined goals are greatly influenced by the organization's dominant culture. The culture of the organization is displayed by the behaviors or actions of the employees, their thoughts and expectations, and the values they espouse in their daily lives. Successful organizations are those that possess and reinforce behaviors that can identify and adapt to change. Leading researchers have defined this type of culture as adaptive or constructive behavioral styles. These behaviors are those found in the organization where employees are able to identify a barrier to progress, and are flexible enough and empowered to make the change to overcome the obstacle. Additionally, a balance exists between accomplishing tasks within specified performance standards and supporting individuals to achieve their best.

Creating an adaptive and constructive organizational culture can be achieved by identifying and removing obstacles that prevent employees from completing tasks at acceptable performance levels, and developing and empowering employees. Barriers and other obstacles can be found in the way the organization is structured, how jobs are designed, how individuals are selected, the type of information that can be accessed and shared, and their ability to effectively problem-solve and make decisions.

The integrated performance matrix and approach described in this book provides the focus, defines the activities and identifies the tools to effectively align the organization's culture to achieve continued success to adapt to the changing environment.

Appendix

Appendix A: Activities Per Track

		People and Organization Alignment
K	♥	**Change Champion** Lead and direct the people in the organizational change track
Q	♥	**Core Values** Identify what is important to the organization
J	♥	**Change Vision** Describe how the organization will look in the future
10	♥	**Guiding Principles** The ideology that will guide the change
9	♥	**Goal Setting** Establish clear goals for the change initiative
8	♥	**Performance Metrics** Identify the key metrics that will measure the change
7	♥	**Inter-unit Coordination** Develop collaboration between business units and departments
6	♥	**Organizational Structure** Examine how employees work together within a team environment
5	♥	**Job/Position Design** Create autonomy, significance, variety and influence
4	♥	**Role Competencies** Define new competencies for each role
3	♥	**Job Fit and Selection** Select employees that fit to the newly defined role
2	♥	**Individual Competencies** Measure and develop individual competencies for the role / position
A	♥	**Rewards and Recognition** Identify and implement a system that promotes new behaviors that align with the organizational change

		Business Process Management
K	♣	**Change Champion** Lead and direct the development of the business processes track
Q	♣	**Value Chain** Identify and define the value chain
J	♣	**Business Policies and Rules** Identify internal controls that may influence the change
10	♣	**Compliance** Identify regulatory and industry compliance areas
9	♣	**High-Level Business Requirements** Identify the necessities needed to support the business
8	♣	**Identify and Document Key Business Processes** Ensure standards are maintained
7	♣	**Analyze Business Processes** Identify value to the customers by reducing non-value added activities
6	♣	**Identify Business Rules** Rules are the process gatekeepers that need to be incorporated in the process
5	♣	**Detailed Business Requirements** Identify those conditions that support the specific details within the process
4	♣	**Identify Activities and Tasks** Define the actions that need to be performed by the job role/ position
3	♣	**Work Steps** Define the steps to perform the activity consistently
2	♣	**Documented Procedures** Establish the correct method of performing the activity
A	♣	**Business Activity Monitoring** Observe changes in requirements from the customer and the business

		Information and Knowledge Management
K	♦	**Change Champion** Lead and direct the knowledge management track
Q	♦	**Taxonomy/ Folksonomy of Content** Develop the methodology to classify content, build naming conventions, and categorize data
J	♦	**Social Networking Philosophy** Crate a method of augmenting official channels of communication to connect with customers
10	♦	**Knowledge Management Framework** Develop the principles and rules to capture and develop knowledge within the organization
9	♦	**Knowledge Development** Create the work environment and align the systems to develop and manage knowledge
8	♦	**Knowledge Acquisition** Define the source of knowledge and determine how it is acquired
7	♦	**Knowledge Deployment** Develop an approach to share knowledge throughout the organization
6	♦	**Reporting and Analytics** Identify metrics and predictive models, then develop tools and techniques to measure performance
5	♦	**Collaboration** Create a work environment to achieve a common business goal, and encourage open communication and collaborative problem-solving
4	♦	**Organization and Team Learning** Create an iterative process that promotes risk taking, sharing information and constructive feedback
3	♦	**Individual Learning** Fulfill the gaps between current individual competencies and the requirements of the role, then develop a plan to foster growth and development
2	♦	**Internalization** Implement a process to align organizational beliefs, attitudes and values with individuals within the organization
A	♦	**Problem-Solving and Decision-Making** Create processes, tools and techniques that will improve decision-making and the quality of decisions

		Technology Alignment
K	♠	**Change Champion** Lead and direct the technology track
Q	♠	**Technical Architectural Principles** Define the general rules and guidelines for the use and deployment of all IT resources and assets within the enterprise
J	♠	**Cloud Computing** Leverage the capabilities of cloud computing to expand mobility
10	♠	**Business Continuity and Disaster Recovery** Build, test and validate continuity and recovery processes, systems and resources
9	♠	**Enterprise Systems** Leverage the integration and collaboration capabilities of systems to support processes
8	♠	**Networks and Infrastructure** Build services that will support business demands and future growth
7	♠	**Technical Compliance** Implement and validate compliance requirements
6	♠	**Application Functions/Modules** Configure the application to enhance business processes incorporating best practices
5	♠	**Mobility and Accessibility** Provide access to systems and information based upon business needs
4	♠	**Technical support** Develop processes and resources to meet the needs of the business during transformational change
3	♠	**Application Configuration** Configure the application to meet the unique business requirements
2	♠	**Interfaces** Link applications and databases in order to share information
A	♠	**Functional Parameters** Define the type of data and naming convention to standardize the task

Appendix B: Defining a Change Champion

What is a Change Champion?

A change champion is a recognized leader within the organization and selected as a person who leads a specific track of work by championing the change, and managing and planning its implementation in coordination with the project team. The champion must understand the reasoning behind the change, and help to communicate the excitement, possibilities and details of the change to others within the organization, as well as lead the team to complete the assigned tasks within the track of work. A change champion is a liaison between the project and the business. He or she represents the interest of their business to ensure that the change occurs with minimal disruption.

A change champion lives in the future, not the present. Regardless of what is going on today within the business, a change champion conveys the vision of the project — what could or should be — and uses that information as the governing sense of action. To a certain extent, a change champion identifies the actual or potential issues with what they see around them within their business unit or department, in favor of a much better vision of the future, and conveys it to the project organizational change management team to be addressed. Then the change champion will convey the designed solutions back to their business unit for implementation. This iterative process will ensure open communications between the various business units and the change project team.

A change champion is fueled by passion and inspires passion in others. Change is hard work and can take a lot of energy. The change champion should not underestimate this. People find comfort in a routine at work. They know what an acceptable standard of work is and find reassurance in their network of support. Without passion, it is very difficult to muster up enough energy to assault the fortress of the status quo that seems to otherwise carry the day.

A change champion has a strong ability to self-motivate. There will be many days where everyone around does not understand and will not offer props. The change champion needs to find it within themselves to get up every day, come to work, and risk being misunderstood and unappreciated, knowing that the real validation may be far in the future and may be claimed by someone else.

A change champion must understand people. At the end of the day, change is about altering people's attitudes and behavior. People will only act if they are motivated to do so. They must feel a sense of urgency, either through the threat of fear or a passion to do things in a better way. Change wil really "stick" when people embrace it. Therefore, change is part sales, part counseling and part encouragement. It's all about people.

	Change Champion Assessment Read each statement, then evaluate the degree in which the change champion behaves.							
1	Is extremely competent in their duties	①	②	③	④	⑤	⑥	Is considered less than competent in their present job duties
2	Is perceived by others as confidant and trusted	①	②	③	④	⑤	⑥	Is a person who distances him or herself from others
3	Enjoys a high degree of credibility with others	①	②	③	④	⑤	⑥	Enjoys only a moderate degree of credibility with others
4	Does not have a history of problems with the organization that would generate a liability for the project	①	②	③	④	⑤	⑥	Has a history of problems within the organization that may generate a liability for the project
5	Has earned the trust and respect of others	①	②	③	④	⑤	⑥	May not be trusted or respected by others
6	Has prior education and/or experience as a facilitator	①	②	③	④	⑤	⑥	Has limited education and/or experience as a facilitator
7	Demonstrates advanced listening skills	①	②	③	④	⑤	⑥	Has not yet demonstrated advanced listening
8	Demonstrates advanced interpersonal communication skills	①	②	③	④	⑤	⑥	Has not yet demonstrated interpersonal communication skills
9	Demonstrates advanced conflict management skills	①	②	③	④	⑤	⑥	Does not demonstrate basic group conflict management skills
10	Demonstrates advanced group dynamic and facilitation skills	①	②	③	④	⑤	⑥	Does not demonstrate basic group dynamic and facilitation skills

11	Is able to conduct effective presentations before a group of peers	①	②	③	④	⑤	⑥	Finds it difficult to conduct effective presentations before peer groups
12	Is willing and able to confront difficult issues and play "hardball" when necessary	①	②	③	④	⑤	⑥	Is often unable or unwilling to confront difficult issues or play "hardball" when necessary
13	Has advanced working knowledge of how people and organizations manage change	①	②	③	④	⑤	⑥	Does not possess a basic working knowledge of how people and organizations change and resist change
14	Demonstrates strong self confidence	①	②	③	④	⑤	⑥	Seems to lack self-confidence
15	Can show empathy without losing objectivity	①	②	③	④	⑤	⑥	Cannot show empathy without losing objectivity
16	Maintains an image of confidentiality, trust and loyalty toward key people in the organization	①	②	③	④	⑤	⑥	Does not maintain an image of confidentiality, trust and loyalty toward key people in the organization
17	Is able and willing to delegate or transfer some portion of current duties to act as a change champion	①	②	③	④	⑤	⑥	Is unable or unwilling to delegate or transfer some portion or current duties to act as a change champion
18	Is knowledgeable about the organization's history and culture	①	②	③	④	⑤	⑥	Is not familiar with the organization's history or culture
19	Is persuasive in presenting his/her point of view	①	②	③	④	⑤	⑥	Is not persuasive in presenting their viewpoint
20	Has a strong desire to take an active part of the change initiative	①	②	③	④	⑤	⑥	Does not desire to take an active role in the change initiative

Scoring

1. Total the responses to all items.
2. Divide the total by 20.
3. Multiply the results by 6 to determine the change champion potential factor.

Low Risk High Potential		Caution Moderate Potential		High Risk Low Potential	
①	②	③	④	⑤	⑥

Low Risk/High Potential: This category reflects a high degree of leadership experience and credibility required to successfully perform as a change champion. The leadership should support this by removing potential barriers and delegating assigned work as needed to support the change initiative.
Caution/Moderate Potential: This category demonstrates a moderate potential to be a change champion. Specific competency gaps should be identified, and a develop plan should be created to maximize potential and minimize specific concerns. Ongoing monitoring of his/her performance and development will be required.
High Risk/Low Potential: This category demonstrates a low potential for performing as a change champion. Longer-term development skills, experience and credibility would be required to remedy this weakness that would not meet the high demands of this change initiative.

Change Champion Characteristics

Plot the answers to each question above to each characteristic. This will indicate the competencies that require development.

		Low Risk/ High Potential	Caution/ Moderate Potential	High Risk/ Low Potential
1	Current competency	① ②	③ ④	⑤ ⑥
2	Value	① ②	③ ④	⑤ ⑥
3	Credibility	① ②	③ ④	⑤ ⑥
4	History of conflict	① ②	③ ④	⑤ ⑥
5	Trust and respect	① ②	③ ④	⑤ ⑥
6	Facilitator education	① ②	③ ④	⑤ ⑥
7	Listening skills	① ②	③ ④	⑤ ⑥
8	Communication	① ②	③ ④	⑤ ⑥
9	Conflict management	① ②	③ ④	⑤ ⑥
10	Group dynamics	① ②	③ ④	⑤ ⑥
11	Presentation	① ②	③ ④	⑤ ⑥
12	Confrontation	① ②	③ ④	⑤ ⑥
13	Change knowledge	① ②	③ ④	⑤ ⑥
14	Strong ego	① ②	③ ④	⑤ ⑥
15	Empathy	① ②	③ ④	⑤ ⑥
16	Confidentiality	① ②	③ ④	⑤ ⑥
17	Availability	① ②	③ ④	⑤ ⑥
18	Knowledge	① ②	③ ④	⑤ ⑥
19	Persuasive	① ②	③ ④	⑤ ⑥
20	Desire	① ②	③ ④	⑤ ⑥

Appendix C: The Integrated Performance Matrix

	People / Organization	Business Process	Technology	Information / Knowledge Management
Strategic Level 1	1. Core Values 2. Change Vision 3. Guiding Principles	1. Value Chain 2. Business Policies and Rules 3. Compliance	1. Technical Architectural Principles 2. Cloud Computing 3. Business Continuity and Disaster Recovery	1. Taxonomy and Folksonomy of Content 2. Social Networking Philosophy 3. Knowledge Management Framework
Tactical Level 2	1. Goal Setting 2. Performance Metrics 3. Inter-Unit Coordination	1. High-Level Business Requirements 2. Identify and Document Key Business Processes 3. Analyze Business Processes	1. Enterprise Systems 2. Networks & Infrastructure 3. Technical Compliance	1. Knowledge Development 2. Knowledge Acquisition 3. Knowledge Deployment
Operational Level 3	1. Organizational Structure 2. Job / Position Design 3. Role Competencies	1. ID Business Rules 2. Detailed Business Requirements 3. Identify Activities and Tasks	1. Application Functions and Modules 2. Mobility and Accessibility 3. Technical Support	1. Reporting and Analytics Collaboration 2. Organizational and Team Learning
Functional Level 4	1. Job Fit and Selection 2. Individual Competencies 3. Rewards and Recognition	1. Worksteps 2. Documented Procedures 3. Business Activity Monitoring	1. Application Configuration 2. Interfaces 3. Functional Parameters	1. Individual Learning and Development 2. Internalization 3. Problem-Solving and Decision-Making

About the Author

George B. Lampere, Ph.D., is a practitioner of business transformation and organizational change management. He has gained his experience over the past thirty years as a consultant working in a wide range of industries. George prides himself on participating in the leading business techniques as they evolved, including total quality management, business process reengineering, Six Sigma, metrics management, organizational change management, organizational culture assessment and alignment, and knowledge management. For an organization to be successful and maintain its competitive advantage, he learned that they must integrate and align their people, processes, technologies and knowledge. Being able to actually achieve this integration is complex and challenging. This book was written in response to this issue.

George B. Lampere was granted a Doctorate degree in Organizational Behavior from Southwest University, a Master's degree in Human Resources Management and Development, and a Bachelor's degree in Management from National-Louis University. His research is used to develop or refine a technique that accelerates the change process providing value.

Dr. Lampere resides with his wife, Jo-Ellen, and his two children, Jill and Ben, and their dog, Bueller in the Chicago area. Additional information on Dr. Lampere can be found at www.GLampere.com.

Index

A

Abilities, *56, 58, 60, 179, 185, 197*
Acceptance, *38, 93, 192, 214*
Accessibility, *79, 123, 134, 136,*
Accomplishment, *6, 64-65, 171, 195*
Accuracy, *121, 127, 148, 174*
Achievement, *42, 55, 67, 105, 195*
Activities and Tasks, *83, 87, 89, 95,*
96, 105, 106, 133, 174, 199,
202-206, 222
Adaptability, *15-16*
ADDIE, *183-184*
Advancement, *55, 61*
Alignment, *17, 23, 29, 31-32, 34, 59-*
60, 103, 108-109, 141, 150, 157, 164
Alliance, *166, 168*
Application Configuration, *140, 224*
Application Functions, *22, 131, 224*
Approval, *16, 98, 104, 135, 141*
Assessments, *48, 75, 106, 129*
Assumptions, *42, 96, 167, 188, 201*
Asynchronous Collaboration, *176*
Attitudes, *60, 186, 196*
Attributes, *31, 140, 142, 153*
Audits, *80, 128-129*
Authority, *18, 48, 98, 192, 199*
Automation, *46, 53, 109, 124, 131,*
210, 214
Autonomy, *51-55, 170*
Availability, *79, 116, 127, 182*
Awareness, *56, 157, 181*

B

BAM (See Business Activity
Monitoring)
Barriers, *23, 42-50, 106, 189, 212*
Baseline, *78, 113, 209*
Behavior, *4, 6, 31, 48-49, 61, 66, 90-*
91, 150, 153, 160, 205
Beliefs, *6, 16, 30, 32-33, 37-38, 61,*
90, 156, 164, 169-171, 176, 186
Benchmarks, *78, 103, 198*
Benefits, *44, 112, 116, 131, 146, 150,*
156-157, 187
Blueprint, *112-114, 145*
Boundaries, *31, 60, 170, 179*
206
Bureaucracy, *5, 46, 48, 60*
Business Activity Monitoring, *105,*
222
Business Continuity, *68, 79, 84, 108,*
119-121, 129-130, 224
Business Policies, *53, 74-75, 85, 212,*
222
Business Processes, 16-22, 47-51, 57,
58, 68-72, 77, 79-89, 105-109, 115,
119-123, 127, 130-132, 135, 138,
140-141, 147, 151, 154, 165, 170,
180, 183, 190-191, 203, 209-210,
213, 227
Business Requirements, 23, 53, 81-
83, 92-94, 96, 103, 108, 111, 113,
116, 127, 132, 148
Business Rules, 5, 59, 74-76, 83, 85,
88, 90, 91, 93, 103, 104, 147, 222

G

Globalization, *122*
Goal Setting, *40-42, 188, 221*
Governance, *77, 80, 82, 112, 159, 174*
Growth, *55, 72, 113, 125, 165, 170, 182, 196*
Guidance, *29, 36, 58-59, 70, 76, 91, 104, 111, 137, 152*
Guidelines, *74, 85, 90-91, 102-104, 112, 118, 126, 132, 184*
Guiding Principles, *27, 37-39, 43, 51, 69, 110, 150, 209, 212*

H

Hardware, *108, 115, 125-126*
Headcount, *14, 51, 54, 60*
Hierarchy, *48, 205*
High-Level Business Requirements, *53, 81, 83, 93, 209, 213, 222*

I

IaaS, *115, 118, 125*
Idea, *103, 135, 186-187, 197*
Identification, *30, 80, 85, 98, 103, 118, 156, 170*
Illustrate, *84, 98, 208*
Implement, *27, 65, 69, 93, 109, 113, 122, 125, 128, 156, 186*
Implementation, *75, 78, 122, 125, 183, 186, 214*
Importance, *44, 57, 71, 102, 161, 188*
Improvement, *21, 73, 124, 132, 171, 174, 188, 196*
Incentives, *41, 65, 160-161*
Inconsistencies, *89*

Independent, *64, 81*
Indicators, *21, 41, 43-44, 68, 82, 87-89, 91, 94, 96, 99-100, 105-106, 175, 192, 213*
Individual Competencies, *62, 192, 221, 223*
Individual Development, *183*
Individual Learning, *62, 63, 182, 185, 223*
Inefficiencies, *21, 105*
Influencers, *150, 162*
Informal, *34-35, 66, 74, 158, 167, 183*
Information, *17, 21, 23, 73, 107, 123, 149, 163, 165, 187, 206, 208, 212-213*
Infrastructure, *115, 125-126*
Innovation, *15, 171*
Insights, *3, 105, 164, 199*
Integration, *16, 47, 73, 109, 113-114, 122, 131-132, 140, 190, 205, 214*
Integrity, *118, 126, 195-197*
Intelligence, *56, 72, 110, 122, 151, 164, 175, 185*
Inter-unit Coordination, *46-49, 51, 221*
Interaction, *55, 157, 163, 165, 170, 181*
Interdependencies, *46, 181*
Interest, *154, 178, 181*
Interface, *125, 143-145*
Internalization, *162, 186, 223*
Interview, *61, 75, 78*
Intuition, *160, 166-167*
Investment, *44-45, 134, 158*
Ishikawa *(See Fishbone)*
Issue, *77, 91, 138, 170, 190-191*

J

Job Fit, *59-61, 63, 221*
Job/Position Design, *53-55*
Journey, *35, 210, 214*
Judgment, *196-197*

K

Kano Model, *167*
Key Business Process, *72, 84, 222*
Kirkpatrick, *183-184*
Knowledge Acquisition, *166-168*
Knowledge Deployment, *169-172*
Knowledge Development, *163-165*
Knowledge Management
Framework, *159-162*
KPI, *43, 82, 87-89, 96, 106, 138*
KSI, *43*

L

Label, *44, 153, 155*
Labor, *35, 53-54, 119*
Leadership, *72, 195-198*
Leading, *188, 216*
Learning, *25, 62, 64, 150, 179-181, 185*
Legacy, *123, 195*
Lessons, *102, 106, 149, 179, 181, 195*
Leverage, *115-116, 122-123, 129, 140, 143, 151, 154, 169*
Limitations, *48, 94, 109, 116*
Linkages, *72-73*
Location, *54, 104, 135, 137, 176*
Loyalty, *196, 203, 205*

M

Maintenance, *121, 128, 130, 132*
Manager, *6, 13, 18, 48, 51, 56, 124*
Mapping, *71, 144, 150, 160, 174, 177*
Market, *21, 35, 88, 153, 167, 180, 190*
Matrix, *17, 167, 231*
Measurement, *44, 60, 105, 160, 162, 164*
Measures, *29-30, 43-45, 62-64, 70, 78, 107, 111, 118, 130, 152, 155, 161, 177, 180, 183, 190, 215*
Media, *156-157*
Methodology, *149, 153, 195*
Methods, *6, 55, 63, 94, 102, 107, 110, 151, 167, 176, 181, 183-185*
Metric, *28, 31, 41, 43-45, 69, 85, 110, 127, 151*
Milestones, *65, 210, 215*
Mission, *28, 69, 110, 151*
Mobility, *53, 79, 83, 115, 126, 130, 134-136*
Models, *50, 112, 115, 118, 130, 164, 173, 181, 185*
Modules, *124, 131, 140, 142*
Morale, *14, 38, 41, 51, 59, 67*
Motivation, *65, 67, 198, 203*

N

Narrative, *84, 86, 89, 98*
Networks, *109, 115, 120, 125, 137-139, 150, 224*
Networking, *64, 90, 92, 115, 125, 150-151, 153-154, 156-158, 180, 212*
Norms, *31-32, 47*

O

Objectives, *18, 29, 41, 51, 65, 81, 95, 100, 112, 141, 143-144, 151, 169, 180, 185, 195-196, 198*

Observation, *75, 105, 149, 164, 167*

Obstacle, *186, 216*

Offering, *35, 131, 137*

Online, *7, 104, 109, 135, 137*

Operational, *15, 43, 50-51, 53, 56, 73, 76, 90, 92, 95, 102, 106, 131-134, 137, 139, 171, 173, 176-177, 179, 183, 208*

Opportunities, *21, 27-29, 35, 55, 63, 69-70, 110-111, 124, 152, 158, 167, 169, 172, 185, 187, 189*

Optimization, *128-129*

Order, *13, 15-16, 28, 46, 52, 56-57, 67, 70, 73, 76, 83-84, 95, 110, 117, 134, 143, 145, 151, 156, 169, 176, 181-182, 185, 200, 203, 205-206*

Organizational Learning, *179-181*

Organizational Structure, *28, 49-50, 52-53, 57-59, 120, 129-130, 161, 195, 206, 221*

Organizations, *5, 104, 117, 128-130, 150, 157-158, 173*

P

Pain, *8-9, 27, 38, 69, 110, 201*

Parameter, *146-148*

Participation, *63, 184, 215*

Partnership, *176-177*

Penalties, *117, 128*

Perception, *73, 145, 166, 170, 179, 181*

Performance Metrics, *43, 49k 58, 62-64, 83, 106, 138, 170, 180, 213, 221*

Personality, *60, 178, 185, 191, 199*

Perspective, *15, 72-73, 82, 90, 92, 112, 131, 133, 164*

Phase, *120-121*

Philosophy, *156-158, 212*

Plans, *18, 120-121, 126, 129-130, 138-139, 145, 160, 200, 205*

Platform, *108, 115*

Policies, *5-6, 32, 38, 47, 53, 59, 74-76, 78, 82, 85, 90, 102-104, 146-147, 155, 158, 161, 212*

Position, *33, 53, 56-62, 80, 95, 172, 181*

Potential, *29-30, 42, 70, 74, 98, 111, 120, 128, 132, 152, 157, 175, 177, 201, 204, 214*

Power, *13, 15, 36, 101, 116-117, 160, 178, 199*

Pressure, *4, 173*

Prime Activities, *208-210, 212-213*

Principles, *37, 112-113*

Problem-Solving, *16, 17, 30, 131, 153, 165, 171, 173, 176, 179, 190-193, 223*

Procedure, *84, 95, 103-104*

Process, *23, 39, 68, 85, 120, 135, 144, 188, 206, 208, 212-213*

Product, *6, 41, 47, 55, 64, 72, 85-87, 92-93, 95-97, 156, 167, 175*

Productivity, *23, 46, 51, 59, 67, 134-135*

Profit, *13, 42, 44-45, 52, 71, 175*

Programs, *21, 66, 125, 143, 165, 179*

Protection, *118, 136*

Psychometric, *60-61*

To aid in the facilitation and implementation of the Business Cards approach I have made available custom printed playing cards, posters and other materials. Order these from my website at www.glampere.com, or contact me at glampere@glampere.com.